Rhetoric, Language, and Reason

Literature & Philosophy

A. J. Cascardi, General Editor

This series publishes books in a wide range of subjects in philosophy and literature, including studies of the social and historical issues that relate these two fields. Drawing on the resources of the Anglo-American and Continental traditions, the series is open to philosophically informed scholarship covering the entire range of contemporary critical thought.

Already published:

Rhetoric, Language, *and* Reason

Michel Meyer

The Pennsylvania State University Press
University Park, Pennsylvania

Library of Congress Cataloging-in-Publication Data

Meyer, Michel.
    Rhetoric, language, and reason / Michel Meyer.

        p.   cm.—(Literature and philosophy)
    Includes bibliographical references and index.
    ISBN 0-271-01057-6—ISBN (invalid) 0-271-01058-4
(pbk.)
    1. Rhetoric. 2. Language and languages—Philosophy.
3. Reasoning. 4. Meaning (Philosophy). 5. Knowledge, Theory of.
6. Problem solving. I. Title. II. Series.
P301.M43   1994
808'.001—dc20   92-41696
                                                                  CIP

Published by The Pennsylvania State University Press,
Barbara Building, Suite C, University Park, PA 16802-1003

It is the policy of The Pennsylvania State University Press to use acid-free paper for
the first printing of all clothbound books. Publications on uncoated stock satisfy the
minimum requirements of American National Standard for Information Sciences—
Permanence of Paper for Printed Library Materials, ANSI Z39.48–1984.

Contents

Acknowledgments

I am grateful to the various editors and publishers who have granted me permission to reprint the following articles: "Toward an Anthropology of Rhetoric" first appeared in *From Metaphysics to Rhetoric*, ed. M. Meyer, trans. Robert Harvey (Dordrecht: Kluwer, 1989), pp. 111–136; "Problematology and Rhetoric" appeared in *Practical Reasoning*, ed. Golden & Pilotta (Dordrecht: Kluwer, 1986), pp. 119–152; "Toward a Rhetoric of Reason" appeared in the *Rhetorical Society Quarterly* (1989): 131–139; "Argumentation in the Light of Theory of Questioning," trans. Marlene Cushman, appeared in *Philosophy and Rhetoric* (1982): 81–103; "The Interrogative Theory of Meaning and Reference" appeared in *Questions and Questioning* (Berlin and New York: De Gruyter, 1986), pp. 341–355; "Science as a Questioning Process: A Prospect for a New Type of Rationality," was published in *Revue Internationale de Philosophie* (1980): 49–89.

In view of the continuity of the volume, some of those papers have been renamed and reworked.

Introduction

This book introduces a new conception of philosophy that I have called *problematology*. As the name suggests, that conception stresses the role and relevance of questioning in the approach to language and reasoning. Problematology is not only the study of questioning but also the analysis of the reasons it has been repressed throughout the history of philosophy. Nonetheless, since Socrates, philosophers and scientists have reasoned by asking questions and by trying to solve them. Questioning has been the unthematized foundation of philosophy and of thought at large, even though philosophers have preferred to adopt another norm, granting privilege to answers and thereby repressing questions into the realm of the preliminary and the unessential.

They did not consider their discursive practice as being articulated upon some question-answer (or problem-solution) complex, but exclusively upon the results they called propositions. Those results were deemed to be self-sufficient or to only refer to one another in an autonomous chain of reasons. Alternatives were excluded by virtue of some propositionalist version of the principle of noncontradiction, claiming that, necessarily, we cannot have both A and not-A, thereby making necessity the guiding norm of reason as manifested in the propositional chain of thought. Nothing problematic or doubtful is allowed in that scheme, if not as a form of ignorance of the propositions which *should*

follow from the previously accepted propositions. The questions that
can emerge must be referred back to those propositions and, as a result,
disappear in them or through them. Logically, it should be the reverse.
The propositions ensue from corresponding questions, not the opposite.

Propositionalism is, of course, based on ontology, which sanctifies the
necessity of what is. Ontology was codified by Aristotle and was assumed until the nineteenth century. Necessity in propositions, truth as
exclusive of all alternative, is guaranteed by the propositional subject:
Socrates could have been tall or not, Greek or not, bald or not, but he
could not have been other than himself, namely, Socrates. But what is he,
if not a set of contingent properties such as those mentioned above?
Propositionalism, in its pursuit of absolute necessity, is then trapped into
difficulties that are all rooted in its ideal of necessity, an ideal which is
itself devoid of necessity and can be logically opposed without contradiction. That difficulty has often been resolved by claiming that there was a
necessity in the principle affirming the necessity of necessity.

Circularity was therefore inevitable. If we analyze it carefully, it is the
very role of the *cogito,* for instance, or of Aristotle's demonstration of
the principle of noncontradiction, to show that the foundation of propositionalism, or apodicticity, does already presuppose that ideal in order
to have such a foundation at all. Foundationalism conceived on those
terms had to die, and it did. But, for that reason, should philosophy as the
search for ultimate principles renounce itself?

In contrast to such a view of reason, we would like to develop another
one rooted in the practice of questioning, a view according to which
propositions are considered as answers. As such, they refer to the questions from which they originate and which give them their meaning, but
they also refer to questions as intrinsic possibilities of alternative thinking on the very matter they deal with. Argument, or rhetoric, far from
being a weak form of thought or inference, a handicapped child of
reason, turns out to be an intrinsic feature of language. It is equal in
dignity to the scientific form of answerhood, from which the problematic aspects of thought, though eliminated as much as possible, are nonetheless dealt with. An answer can suppress the original question, but it
can also pose it afresh for other questioners or suggest new questions,
and even be contested in its very claim of being a solution. It is only in
the propositional model of truth that debate is seen as a lesser form of
rational practice because it places itself at the level of finished results,
which represents a kind of Platonic world and to which most scientists
have renounced. In fact, rationality begins with the formulation of prob-

lems, and it does not reduce itself to the adequacy of response. We have here a pluralistic model of answerhood, in which several genres can coexist without there being any necessity to privilege necessity (or any other type of answer) as being the model for all possible propositions.

What is to be understood by *question* and *problem?* Would a question not be purely and simply a phrase? In fact, *question* extends beyond the realm of language, although the linguistic domain illustrates it well. What happens when one affirms that this or that is in question? What is precisely meant? The response is immediate; an alternative is evoked from the moment we do not specify which question in particular is the point. If, for example, John's visit tomorrow is in question, this implies that John can come or not come. To pose the question or to evoke it assertorically signifies that the speaker wishes to know. It is with this wish that the epistemic connotation is associated—not with what is in question in itself, but with the fact that someone raises the question in one manner or another. The epistemic side of the interrogation conditions the fact that any question on occasion allows itself to be transplanted by the formulation "The question X is about *knowing* whether X."

A definition of the *question* through alternatives demonstrates that the question itself, and not either proposition, constitutes the issue, even though what is under question can be declared assertorically. In general, questions and problems can be identified. If one prefers a psychological definition, one can say that a question is an obstacle, a difficulty, an exigency of choice, and therefore an appeal for a decision. A question is decided by responding to it, linguistically or in other ways. This response implies that there is no question without an answer, and that it is the exigency of questioning, represented by this latter implication, that a global process exists necessarily wherein they refer to one another. Questions, therefore, indicate the presence of a questioning process wherein they are inserted: that is to say, the dynamic of the move to resolution.

The fundamental duality of language is the difference between question and answer, which I have called the *différence problématologique* ("problematological difference"). This difference is at the root of language, for the very reason that language responds to the human problem of which, for instance, dialogical interaction is an essential dimension. Upon this difference are erected such other uses of language as informing, communicating, and persuading. At this level, the problematological difference is embodied in the opposition between the explicit and the implicit; the essence of certain answers is to be explicit. On the other hand, however much the problems are not spoken, they allow for their own expression, and this leaves room for the sort of answer which is, strictly speaking, problematological. All discourse, from the simple phrase to the great text, can thus assure *a priori* the double function of language—namely, to treat the problems posed therein by proposing their solution or by expressing their nature. Therefore, a proposition, a discourse, can mark the question just as well as the solution.

An apocritical expression, i.e., one characterizing a response, while apocritical relative to the question it resolves (for such is the definition of the apocritical character of a proposition of discourse), is equally problematological, i.e., expressive of a question. To what question is an answer related? At first glance, to the question which it resolves. If it resolves the question and if that is the only *relatum* possible, then the answer has only one possible function, the apocritical. Otherwise, the problematological duplication of the question would be its own solution, which goes against the distinction between question and answer; one does not resolve a question by merely stipulating or repeating it. Therefore, the question to which the answer refers (problematologically) differs from the one which it resolves (apocritically).

In sum, problematology wishes to integrate argumentation and logic, figurative and literal language, knowledge and literature, into one overall conception of thinking as it actually takes place, without favoring any specific ontology, nor any other preconceived, unquestioned, *a priori* norm of reason.

Chapter 1 is devoted to the roots and perpetuation of propositionalism. We see that Aristotle codifies its foundations through ontology, but also through the logical principles of any possible thought, as we find them in logic but also in rhetoric. But those principles will reveal themselves without foundation: how could they have any necessity if they are meant to ground it? The Cartesian enterprise should be seen as a response to that difficulty—the *cogito* is supposed to be self-grounding. The goal of providing a necessity to the idea of necessity remains; as a result, propositionalism perpetuates itself in spite of the new foundational role ascribed to subjectivity.

In fact, propositionalism remains questionable, to the extent that it is itself an answer to a problem which paradoxically consists in eradicating questions and questioning, an eradication which leads to apodicticity and unicity and serves as the measure of truth. The original problem that propositionalism purports to face is how to attain apodictic truth, but that quest itself has nothing apodictic and fails to meet its own criterion. Hence the solution which consists in eradicating all reference to problematicity, a procedure which enables the first "answer" to appear as a self-sustaining proposition. The affirmation of the ego by itself belongs to that class of assertions. It is the first answer to be out-of-the-question, beyond doubt, but only because radical doubt is suppressed through its being affirmed in a true statement which in fact asserts that "I doubt" is true each time I proffer it. And if it is an answer, it can be originary only by postulation and negation, for what comes first is questioning itself, as embodied here in the original doubt.

Nineteenth-century philosophy, with Marx, Nietzsche, and Freud, will stress the illusion of the foundational role of subjectivity. The crisis of reason and of foundations will put problematicity to the fore in many areas of thought and culture, ranging from painting to literature, from philosophy to music. The problematic which has emerged as a new reality could only be faced as something negative in regard to the old model, something necessary to supersede and impossible to overcome within the given framework which has engendered such a problematicity. In contrast, problematology emphasizes the *positive* features of what is problematic and shows how questioning is a new starting point. As a result, rhetoric has reemerged as a new form of truth of language and reasoning, the truth of man as an individual. Communication, transcendental or not, reflects the differences between human beings who have to live together. Rhetoric is the mode of expression of those differences, even if argumentation is meant to resolve them by generating some consensus. Man is seen as always changing, historical, other than what he is. He is what he is not and he is not what he is, and this saying of Jean-Paul Sartre suffices to highlight the rhetoric of the ego, which always transforms new questions on the basis and in terms of old answers (to previous questions).

Chapter 2 focuses mainly on the crisis of propositionalism, of its foundations, but also on its evolution in the twentieth century. The "defundamentalization" of the subject has been its main feature, as much as positivism and nihilism have been its ultimate consequences. If everything turns out problematic, the only answer left is that we can no longer state anything but that very "answer." It is the end of philosophy. A path other than nihilism has been positivism: if we wish to reach answers, as science does, we have to imitate and transform philosophy into some science of science. Nihilism and positivism nonetheless profess an unquestioned view of questioning, which still sees its eradication as an ideal and its perpetuation as a weakness, a fault, or nonsense—at any rate, something which cannot be faced in the propositional model of exclusive answerhood-without-questions.

We can only find expressed in literature the emerging problematic
features of our civilization, as an analysis of some of Franz Kafka's work
will exemplify. But questioning has to be faced as such, in order to
understand not only our human condition but also language use and its
rhetoric at large, from politics to psychoanalysis.

Chapter 3 focuses more specifically on the contrast between traditional rhetoric and the rhetoric based on questions and questioning.

In Chapter 4, the aim is to expound the *problematological view of
rhetoric* as a consequence of a theory of language which is itself based on
questioning. When we speak or write, we always have a question in
mind. Either we communicate the answer to that question or we ask the
response from the interlocutor. This (problematological) difference between question and answer commands all the operations of reasoning
and communication through language. Interrogativity leaves its mark in
the various modes and forms of discourse which we call upon, but it also
determines the structure and differences between the rhetorical, dialogical, hermeneutical, and inferential levels of linguistic usage. Rhetoric
emerges as an integrated theory, in which we can capture both the
referential and the literary possibilities of discourse.

Hence Chapter 5, in which the question of meaning is tackled more
specifically. Meaning is an essential problem for the humanities at large;
it is also the meeting point of linguistics and rhetoric. The entities we
should consider are sentences and textual wholes as well, fictional or
not. The question is how to relate fiction to the everyday uses of language. A basic law of fictionality is proposed on the basis of a general
conception of language, a law that will enable us to relate literature to
the other modes of speech, thereby suppressing the gap that has usually
been accepted as prevailing between fiction and referentiality, sentences
and texts.

In conclusion, Chapter 6 raises the question of the language and practice of science. Questioning is constitutive of knowledge, too, which
proceeds by trial and error from problems to be solved. What are the
overall implications of such a view? What can problematology say about
the rationality of science, in contrast to other forms of reasoning, such as
those analyzed previously, like rhetoric or hermeneutic? The problematological difference as it is embodied in the notion of scientific
result grants some autonomy to the discourse of science, which has
served as a basis for seeing truth, and discourse in general, as self-
sufficient in regard to originary questions. Nonetheless, the scientific
process itself is a questioning one, which is articulated upon the relation-

ship between the context of discovery and the context of justification. This difference in context is both logical and genealogical.

Finally, with language, rhetoric, and knowledge accounted for in terms of questioning, a general conception of reason emerges little by little as a response to the foundational crisis that still affects philosophy as a whole. Positivism, which was based on logic, gives way to problematology, which puts forth a new rhetoric whose truth lies in the way in which the problematic is treated rather than in the fashion in which it is solved, if ever. But that treatment is already an answer.

1

The Birth of Propositionalism, and How Ontology Became Anthropology: Aristotle and Descartes

1. FROM ARISTOTLE TO DESCARTES

Aristotle was the first thinker to propose a codification of Western rationality. It is true that Plato, against whom he nevertheless reacted, preceded him on certain points. The predicative theory of judgment gives form to the proposition, while scientific and dialectic syllogistic are the modes of production of propositions. The well-known principle of noncontradiction, which is the key of all argument and of all possible discursivity, is found at the foundation of *logos.* How can such a principle be demonstrated without putting it into practice? Aristotle is without ambiguity: such a justification cannot be furnished without begging the question, for logical demonstration rests on noncontradiction. Thus we have recourse to dialectic: Aristotle will validate his supreme principle by means of a hypothesis which brings to mind Descartes's "Evil Genius" in that he imagines someone contradicting his principle. If this principle cannot be justified directly, it can at least be established indirectly by refuting all possible refutations. The proof *ad absurdum* is an example of good dialectical argument in that, through propositional complementarity, by eliminating one of the branches of the alternative A or non-A, the opposite term necessarily remains. Here we find verified that cherished idea of Aristotle's in which the dialectic can, in some way, be the foundation of the scientific ideal of necessity. According to Aristotle, he who opposes the principle of noncontradiction is in a bad position precisely because he practices what he expressly rejects. By contradicting, he gives credit to noncontradiction, with which, however, he wants nothing to do. The contradiction of the principle of noncontradiction being an untenable position, the principle in question triumphs by evicting the adversary.

One could believe this to be the case at least on a first reading. How could Aristotle's imaginary contradictor be really troubled by his own incoherence given what he affirms about coherence: an affirmation which perpetuates itself as soon as it destroys itself? Propositionalism finds itself once again bereft of foundation. For we must see that Aristotle wished to impose a certain vision of discourse and of reason which we now know was to determine the history of thought up to the present by making judgment the minimal unity, i.e., the measure and the bearer of truth.

The principle of noncontradiction does not just refer to the principle of identity. It also defines the cardinal form of *logos* as proposition, i.e., as a compound containing a subject and a category-attribute. It would be wrong to see in this principle merely a condition for the existence of *logos;* it is in fact much more than that. It characterizes the very structure of propositional discursivity and rationality. Let us examine this more closely. If we affirm something, say B, and can state something else, something different from B to the point of opposition, say non-B, we obtain a real discourse, which implies, of course, the ability to utter more than a single and same thing. Therefore, B as well as non-B must be possible. But this will only be the case if a same subjacent reality is postulated for B and non-B of which it will be said that it *is* B or non-B. The subject will be called A, and B as well as non-B will become categories: the identity (thus the permanence) of A will imply that B and non-B may be said to be in a relation of successive identification with respect to A. A cannot simultaneously be B and non-B if we want A to remain what it is, that is, A. At this point, predication refers to the identity of the subject: predicates and subjects are hardly conceivable without one another. Thanks to this, it can now be maintained without difficulty that contrary assertions are possible if they relate to a subject for which they are the categorization determining it as the subject that it is. By introducing the concept of subject, discourse as a plurality of different and opposed propositions may henceforth be understood without any difficulty. And, as Aristotle was to explain to us in his theory of syllogism, thanks to the implementation of noncontradiction, propositional *logos* is able to generate propositions indefinitely.

Nevertheless, we stumble against this principle as against something obvious. Propositionalism may be contested at its very roots by the philosophical skepticism incarnated in the incoherent contradictor that Aristotle imagines. How are we to face this "Evil Genius" who distills the poison of unsurpassable doubt? How are we to accept the very idea of the ultimate evidence of the first principles of propositionalism? These two questions are, in these very terms, those of Descartes. Descartes is always imagined to be a radical breaker of the tradition that preceded him and as explicitly opposing Aristotle. He is indeed so in regard to syllogistic, but the principles of syllogistic inevitably escape syllogistic because of the inevitable regression *ad infinitum* that would otherwise result from it. As for the break which Descartes introduces, it is perhaps less total than Cartesian doubt would give us to think. What Descartes obviously wants to institute is a foundation of propositional order incarnated in the deductive rationality both of discourse and of mathematics. Since evidence and its corresponding intuition sustain propositionalism, he must show why it is evident that evidence must impose itself as such. We know that Cartesian thought is circular; Descartes puts into practice the *logos* which he wishes to found. He nevertheless gives something like a second life back to propositionalism at the dawn of modern times, that is, at a time which requires exactly the type of adaptation with which he inflects rationality. I will explain. The primacy of consciousness, which is affirmed in the famous *cogito,* has another function than the one that we usually accord to it. We usually associate Descartes with idealism and the birth of the subject. This is all quite true, but it is not all. What does this famous birth of the subject really mean? Is the subject as a foundation not to be found in judgment? Why this anthropological shift? With its automatic syllogisms, the Aristotelian machinery could not integrate the idea of a general mathematization of nature which was echoed by the new science. But it is legitimate to wonder how the unity of Reason could be assured, for all that, by the concept of man as a foundation.

The mathematization of *logos* is not the only thing that must become conceivable according to Descartes. There is also an increased rhetoricization of discourse which acts as a counterbalance to mathematization and which can only kill the scientificity of syllogism which was used by the Scholastics to say everything and anything. Scientific syllogism in Aristotle is opposed to rhetorical practice, thanks notably to ontology. Indeed, when judgment says that a certain A is B, it affirms what A is; and it is because it is necessarily this and nothing else that there is scientific syllogism. The ontological requirement is determinant for the scientificity of syllogism. It is henceforth understood that with univocity and plurivocity of being to found the constraining (or to explain the nonconstraining) character of an argument, the philosopher feels discomfort at facing the necessities of modern science which are not on the order of simple formal logic. But behind the movement of the Renaissance there is more than a requestioning of empty formalism and of the syllogistic ontology inherited from Aristotle and put in the service of theological conceptions of the cosmos. In the background, there is a realization that because everything may be expressed and rejected on opposite grounds, the famous constraining of argument is lost. Noncontradiction is not enough to materialize truth which pertains to another level of research (mathematical and observational perhaps, but certainly not formal, thus ontological in the way the Greeks and the thinkers of the Middle Ages understood it). What is therefore needed is a substance-foundation other than the one that syllogistic sees in subjects of judgment and their purely rhetorical ontological relations. The word is out: once constraining is abandoned, *logos* is no more than rhetoric, and this is exactly what is reproached of Scholasticism. Moreover, there is a whole resurgence of rhetoric in the Renaissance. Michel Foucault has reminded us of the extent to which similarity and resemblance dominated the intellectual processes of the sixteenth century. Descartes was to seek a new substance-subject in order to put an end to the rhetoricization of the *logos* and to give a foundation for that mathematicization of the cosmos which he was to pursue. With resemblance and analogy everything is in everything, everything has a relationship with everything, everything—thus its contrary—can be said. It is bothersome that no answer is excluded, because if a question is asked—an alternative—we should be able to eliminate one term of this alternative in order to give the other term as the answer. Henceforth a question cannot really be resolved; it will be indefinitely arguable if not indefinitely argued. Let it be noted that this destiny is inscribed, independent of the *quodlibet* practiced in the medieval university, in Aristotelian syllogistic itself:

> Aristotle's efforts to establish a theory of science evince . . . more than one difficulty on the essential points. There is a difficulty, first of all, with the very notion of science and with the distinction

between science and dialectic: in the *Topics,* the two disciplines are both contrasted and linked, especially as to the knowledge of principles. And when in the *Analytics* Aristotle returns to this question of principles, he returns also, more or less explicitly, to dialectical processes, thus attempting, over and against his own very clear declarations, to found the necessary upon the probable.[1]

While this separation may well be necessary with Aristotle, it is nonetheless impossible, and contamination between the two is inevitable.

Descartes will thus combat the rhetoricization of *logos,* the fact that questions perpetuate themselves in their answers, which thus only appear to be solutions. Whence the problem of determining what a solution is: this will become the *Discourse on the Method.* Against a certain ontology, a new logic, a new *organon,* must be set up and founded.

In order to discover the model of the out-of-the-question (i.e., the answer) when everything has become problematic (a situation which Descartes sums up for us in his radical doubt and the motivations he provides for it), an answer is necessary which by expressing this universal problematization will suppress it at the same time. This, we know, will be the *cogito.* The affirmation of the primacy of consciousness, of the "I *am* thinking," is the position of an out-of-the-question liable to resolve all debates, all possible questions—an Archimedean fulcrum which will allow one to decide whether an answer is an answer or not. Rhetorical errancy and soft humanism are finished: here is the die-hard [*pure et dure*], thus the scientistic, version of Reason which grants the thinking substance its full role. How will the *cogito* as unquestionable answer found the unity of the new rationality? Through reflexivity, through transference of property, the substance that I am will be the foundation of all substantification, of any subject of judgment, and, finally, of causality itself. What else does Descartes say in the *Third Meditation?*

For example, I think that a stone is a substance, or is a thing capable of existing independently, and I also think that I am a substance. Admittedly I conceive of myself as a thing that thinks and is not extended, whereas I conceive of a stone as a thing that is extended and does not think, so that the two conceptions differ enormously; but they seem to agree with respect to the classification "substance". Again, I perceive that I now exist, and remember that I have existed for some time; moreover, I have various thoughts which I can count; it is in these ways that I acquire the ideas of duration and number which I can then transfer to other things.[2]

This text is of cardinal importance because it illustrates, better than any other, the essence of philosophical reasoning: I am a subject, a substance; there are therefore subjects and substances which correspond to what I can conceive (clearly and distinctly), such as myself. I am the model of the answer because the *I am* is the answer which conditions all other answers, and so on. The answer is deduced each time from its reflexive thematization, which is autonomized by applying it to something else. Such is the meaning of the Cartesian foundation in the principle of reflexivity. This primacy given to anthropological substance restores to inference all of its force by transforming it in the most radical manner of all. From syllogistic, it will become causal. Mechanism is born. It too will become generalized into ontology. How is this movement to be understood? If from A I can say B as well as non-B, then A is identified by an alternative: since it is itself problematical, nothing stops us from saying non-A. The identity of A then indeed creates a problem, and no wave of an ontological wand over a possible arrangement of the meanings of being, aimed at making opposites noncontradictory, will change anything whatsoever as to the reality of things. On the other hand, if I can form the idea of an unquestionable principle, I will have restored to the idea of subject all its force, and judgment—the proposition—will once again have become possible. I will be able to conclude that A is B, A therefore B. Here, the model of the subject of judgment is substance. The inference clutches to a relation of substances—whence mechanism. What is causality if not the fact that A entails B unwaveringly and not non-B?

The certainty of such a shift is reaffirmed and founded in the *cogito,* which is indeed the birth certificate of the causality principle. The experience that the subject has of its own deducibility, caused by the objectivity of the concept of subject which authorizes it to call itself a thinking substance, is the source of all future experience, which can therefore only be causal.

2. THE DEATH OF THE SUBJECT AND THE BIRTH OF MODERNITY

It is the same with subjects as it is with the rest: excess is always harmful [*le trop nuit en tout*]. With Descartes and his successors, the subject is seen as granting subjectivity a founding, constitutive, and (as Kant would say) transcendental role. What did Descartes thus accomplish other than to prevent rhetoric from encroaching upon the entire *logos?* When I say that he sought an answer to every possible question, one must not for an instant think that there is any concern with questioning in Descartes. On the contrary, all he wants is to put a stop to the rhetoricization which consists in questioning without ever being able to answer once and for all. Causality is solution and it is also science. This is sufficient to suppress interrogativity, which is considered a failure of the mind. Besides, what is doubt but an assertive mode of our thinking process? When I *say* to myself "I doubt," Descartes states, I cannot but *conclude* that I am. It is not because I doubt that I am, it is because I can *say* the one that I can *affirm* the other. We never stop affirming—even when we doubt. We do not really question, unless we make a rhetoric of assertivity out of this "questioning," in which case doubt would merely be the rhetorical question referring to the preliminary assertion that I think—the supreme condition of all possible assertivity. Thus no matter what may be said, we always fall back on the subject and its absolute identity: I can say that I am, no matter what problem is posed. The subject prohibits all questions by being *a priori* the ultimate answer before any question is even asked. It is truly that A which subtends B and non-B, the opposite. No other subject has this force, for all can be denied with the exception of the fact that I am, for if I deny, I still think. Every question is necessarily rhetorical in that the subject renders any debate, for which it is not *a priori* the judge, impossible. By anticipation concerning the very nature of the question asked, the subject literally has the answer to everything. The subject is that authority of automatic closure of *logos* upon itself. Judgment ensures its perenniality as absolute model. Once we realize that the Aristotelian subject does not prevent dialectical opposition which can, furthermore, disguise itself in syllogisms (just like any proposition), we understand the deep significance of the anthropological redefinition of the subject, i.e., of the recentering of propositionalism in the classical age. If A is a real subject in a proposition like "A is B," it excludes its opposability, which must confirm its identity. Now, according to Descartes, only the thinking subject possesses this property, since it maintains itself through all negation. On the other hand, nothing prevents a judgment from being handed down upon rhetoricization with the possibility of having non-A with B like A with non-B as well as with B. The subject loses its identity through opposable predication and is no longer really the subject. The Aristotelian subject gives no guarantee of the power to face the rhetoricization of reason, especially as Aristotle accords acceptance to rhetoric and recognizes its right to use syllogism. As judging is nothing other than judging of the permanence of the subject beyond all possible discussion *on* the subject, the rhetoricization of *logos* destroys the idea of subject in its very function. Through the primacy of consciousness, of its necessity and, in general, of the transference through reflexivity of the concept of substance, the subject, born of the thinking subject, once again becomes possible. This subject is then the concept which restores validity to the proposition in which the out-of-question identity of this subject must be ensured.

But the centuries passed, exhausting more and more the resources of Cartesianism. In the nineteenth century, under the critiques of Marx, Nietzsche, Freud, and Darwin, the anthropological primacy collapsed, plunging thought into the confusion of the "trace" and the "lack," whose stigmata contemporary thought still bears in the depths of its irrationalism. How could the shock of history thus break the well-rounded closure of propositional *logos?* All contradictions are reducible if the locking mechanism is automatic: Is not man as a foundation the identical mainstay of any contradictority that may arise? In fact, if it is not recognized that the change must always be integrated from the reduction of permanency which establishes its authority upon this historical becoming, it will not be understood that even though it is closed, the Cartesian model had to, in the end, renounce its theoretically indefinite perpetuation. The latter rests upon the nature of the ego which effects the closure of *logos.* The ego is thus the rhetorical authority through which rhetoric repudiates itself. This may seem a curious remark at first reading. It means that the ego functions by closing *logos* upon itself because it has an answer for everything, for every question. This implies the reducibility of all contradictions to the identical which absorbs them. But the ego cannot admit itself to be a rhetorical authority, because it functions the way it does precisely in order to prevent rhetoric from invading *logos* so as to establish itself as out-of-question before all problematization which should be taken into account as such. The ego must be able to answer everything. But it can succeed in doing so only if it evacuates *a priori* the possibility of having true questions to which, directly or indirectly, it does not have the solution or the resolution. Every problem encountered must be rhetorical in the sense that one usually speaks of the rhetorical question: it must be exclusively a purely formal question, in that it refers back to some preliminary assertion which it carries forward through implication. By denying rhetoric, the ego cannot recognize itself as rhetoric, as something that turns any new question back toward an old one to which it already knows the answer.

Given a question that presents an opposition, the ego that must face this alternative brings it back, by intuition or deduction, to what it is not: a preconstituted solution. This process is well known under the names of rationalization or derivation. The ego suppresses the question which was a real question, resolving it by automatic suppression and thus transforming the dialectical relation instituted by the confrontation with the newness of the real into an implicit confirmation of that which is old; at the same time, the ego represses itself in doing so. Rhetoricization consists in displacing real questions, questions *of* the real, into questions to which one already has (intuition) or can recover (deduction) the answer.

In the ego, the unconscious is problematicity repressed and displaced into rhetorical problems and denied as such. Irreducible problematicity, which weaves the web of the unconscious, manifests itself by a contradictority which is reabsorbed, processed, displaced, and rationalized by the ego in the relation to the real—a problematicity that has its own sources in addition to everything that derives from historicization, that is, from temporalization springing from outer reality which must ceaselessly be refit to its reality coherence as such. It may come as a surprise to read that reality constitutes itself rhetorically. This is not the traditionally held image of the real. Independent from us, solid, invariable, permanent, as well as the cause of many unexpected novelties, the real imposes itself as something that is not of the rhetorical order. However, this image of reality, which we will not contest, is not a given, but the result of a process that involves the ego. The ego is confronted with problems, alternatives, and contradictions which it must answer. Opposition only makes sense with respect to answers which are already granted, at least some of which are imbedded in the far reaches of ourselves, doubtlessly to our great relief. The continuity of the world requires precisely that any new question be reducible to an old one; if not, we will be confronted with a conflict which *for me* is insoluble and the world will appear shattered [*se présentera en rupture*]. The continuous identity of reality therefore means nothing other than the assimilation of the new— of difference—to identity (which really is not identity except rhetorically) through displacement which translates the problematic into the nonproblematic, the unknown into the already known (or the knowable). It is not that we cannot accept the irreducible newness, but we must always be able to express it in relation to that which it is not in order to accept it as it is. This supposes a rhetorical transformation that rationalizes and recovers the opposition, turning it into a question that the ego can discuss—a rhetorical question. Let us understand one another well: if the real can appear to the ego as it is—renewed, unexpected, and identical in its solidity outside the subject—it is because the subject rhetoricizes and rationalizes the information, that is, coordinates it and, quite simply, names it and thus recognizes it. When we affirm that reality is constituted rhetorically, it is not a matter of content but of form, of the very possibility of a real which is stable because it is so treated by the ego. In order for the real to indeed be the real, this rhetoric of the subject must be repressed by it. This entails a derhetoricization of reality which imposes itself in its objective identity. All of this follows from the fact that we must resolve the problems of existence, life, and survival, and that this ceaseless questioning of ourselves has to be elaborated collectively as well as individually, based on the experience of past resolutions, based upon the quasi-automatic suppression of the destabilization caused by the problematization of our commerce with the world. This problematization is, I repeat, not independent of us, for the problem only exists in relation to us. Once it is evacuated and rhetoricized by the ego, the solution asserts itself as being independently valid, without any further reference to the problematic, i.e., to that which moves us and situates the real in relation to us. If the conscious ego is often likened to the act of taking charge of the real, it can only be so once the relation between them is already played out, when they can be posited separately. Idealism and empiricism have defined themselves on the basis of the moment of which we speak, in order to reflect upon the subject's possibility to leave himself in order to approach the object and constitute it in its objectivity. Both were destined to fail because they posed a process-problem based on the results of that process. Thinking only in terms of results, idealism could no more retrieve the object than empiricism could the subject. Subject and object being separated for both idealism and empiricism, the question of the process of knowledge became insoluble. How could the real emerge from the ego? How can the real engender its own perception, thus its own fracture? In short, the implications of the affirmation that the ego integrates the real into its own independence are too often forgotten. And the implications are ideologization as well as all less specific forms of rationalization by which the reality of the real arises [*surgit*] while concealing something from us: an irreducibility that would destabilize us. In order for the ego to accept the real as is, its looming appearance [*surgissement*] must be rhetoricized—an appearance which introduces difference or alterity: the question which, in the final analysis, is an "I question *myself*" [*je m'interroge*], since in it I am always in some way put back into question.

Of course, there is still science: one tends to think that by accepting the newness of experience in its very irreducibility, it states the real nonrhetorically. Here, once again, one must be careful with respect to inherited images. A theory is rarely abandoned because of the authority of problems challenging it. A purely ad hoc process of integration and of partial revision takes place well before scientists, who have judged a theory irremediable, decide to abandon it for another. Resistance to problematization is to be found in science just as it is in the rest of our intellectual pursuits. In order to save a certain image of the real, science rhetoricizes questions by various means that range from neglect to conventional explanation through the declaration of irrelevance and factual minimalization without forgetting the challenging of factual interpretation which cannot be dissociated from the latter. Moreover, the ego also ends up rejecting rationalizations which open onto incoherence and the inassumable just as it does onto the increasing impossibility to take into account new realities on the basis of old ones.

The ego, the subject, is the authority which mediates between our corporeality, our instincts, our problematicity (in the broad sense), and that which is outside and opposes itself to the free flow of solutions which an inertia of our inner tendencies would find natural to put into practice. The world is only a problematizing one because it checks these solutions. The unconscious is woven with problems because the solution to them is impossible, in consideration of the *fact* that we are in the midst of things and beings, that life is not self-evident, and that, consequently, the unconscious exists as insurmountable problematicity. Between this problematicity and that which puts us back into question from the outside (but in the early times, this in the same thing), there is the ego.

The closure of the ego corresponds to the necessity of facing all problematization which emerges both from the depths of our being and from outside necessities. It is easy to imagine that the equilibrium is fragile and that any pressure that is too strong from either side could entail breakages. To avoid this, the ego closes itself [*se clôture*], thus managing to live in a world which seems essentially stable to it. The infinite resolutive capacity of *logos* derives from this. But the infinitude of this automatism in resolution denies itself. Hence, the unconscious is the human condition of reality. The ego must repress the part of itself which represses the problematic—suppressing the latter and turning it into ready-made or fast answers. It must be the answering process and by itself respond to questions which cannot really be posed. In brief, the ego is rhetorical in order to combat rhetoric, in order to provide itself a real. Because this rhetorical component cannot be expressed, it must be occulted. This explains the repression which splits the subject into conscious ego and unconscious ego. The Cartesian subject is only a subject in that it answers all possible questions ahead of time, thus to the extent that it places itself beyond all debates in the capacity of outside-the-debate. But the rhetoricization of all new problems in the uninterrupted continuity of subjectivity is hidden by the apodictic character of the affirmation of this subjectivity. One gets the feeling that science fulfills this rhetorical role while, at the same time, denying it. Consciousness, as it was to define modern subjectivity, was to allow rhetoric to function without having to be expressed as such. Once the breaking down of subjectivity as foundation was consummated in radical problemati-zation, consciousness could not continue to cover the totality of the subject. And the unconscious emerged as the other side of the mirror—as negation of consciousness—with all of its rhetorical properties of condensation and displacement. The resurgence of rhetoric in the twen-tieth century has no other origin than the crisis of the subject. Psycho-analysis was to be the *avant-garde* of this renewal. It arises when we become aware of the role played by the rhetorical component of the ego which closes its *logos.* But because it is not the Cartesian master of it, the ego cannot help but let this rhetoric appear as what it is. The subject is then unmasked. Rhetoric will not really be studied for itself until later. Through recognition of the role of rhetoric, the subject both saves and loses itself. As a Cartesian subject, the human subject, which is founda-tional, is dead; but, as an open articulation of the problematic, the sub-ject can be understood to be at the crux of a new anthropology, even though the very problematic which concerns it cannot be thought of as such, precisely because there is no problematology as yet. Rhetoric remains understood under the definition which Plato and Aristotle, then Chaim Perelman, preserved for it (i.e., the contradictority of proposi-tions) and not as a referral to a question which alone allows us to apprehend why, and in relation to what, opposition is possible.

The defundamentalization of the subject defines postmodernity in all its aspects. It means that man is no longer Descartes's and Kant's "pure subject" in relation to which man is always something else. Vanity, ac-cording to Thackeray, or consciousness, according to Sartre: to be what one is not, and not to be what one is. Far from being able to resolve everything yet, the subject thus becomes, in turn, a problem (A and non-A) like anything else. Empiricism has taken over man, who is like any object: the human sciences have become possible. But the bell tolls also for the preeminence of moral values which are rooted in man. Barbarity is not far off. But let us not misinterpret Nietzsche and Heidegger. What it is necessary to see clearly is that the problematization of the subject

cannot be conceived as such, as long as we remain within the propositional model of *logos*, though it be without foundation. Utilitarianism,
Darwinism, and pragmatism will be seen as sufficient and will "validate"
such a *logos*, which no longer maintains itself except by its tradition and
efficacy. The problematic will be the inexpressible destiny of this *logos*;
but it is a *logos* which only knows the positivity of the assertorial, or,
more precisely, can express and state only this positivity, even if it realizes that there are hollows in it. Henceforth, the problematization which
affects the out-of-the-question which we were will still be thought according to propositional rationality which, for want of a foundation,
cannot but open onto irrationalism. Heidegger, like Ludwig Wittgenstein, will speak of silence. Sartre will continue to stake everything on
consciousness and the *cogito* but would be forced to insert alterity into
the very definition he gives; this would lead him to the analysis of what
he calls "bad faith." Jacques Derrida will treat man as a trace—but a trace
of what? The ascendancy of the Cartesian subject and of the propositional model thus endures through its very negation. As for Jacques
Lacan, he will make the subject the empty compartment in the network
of signifiers—a lack which is never filled. Derrida calls it *différance*, for
this discrepancy of the self with itself is the essence of the subject.
Structuralism encloses the subject in a network of which it is no longer
the master: a Borgesian labyrinth in which it is lost and indefinitely
searches for itself as a consciousness (a consciousness being, of course,
consciousness of itself and not unconscious)—it is fundamentally its
own mirror. It *was*, one should say more precisely, and all this is what
these authors remind us. Man cannot be any of this anymore, but what
he is cannot be uttered, since he is what he is not—he is to the extent
that he is always something other than himself. The irreversible course
of time in which man is projected, transcendence, all of these words
hide poorly (behind their manifest truth) what they borrow from a past
whose supersession can only be conceived in terms that prevent this
supersession from taking place. We indeed remain within a mode of
thought that we would like to evacuate but cannot. Problematicity is not
approached otherwise than by alterity, contradiction, and the temporality which maintains the oppositions without incoherency, as the formulation of the principle of noncontradiction indicates. The time and the cult
of tradition, which cannot but must be superseded [*indépassable mais à
dépasser*], are thus found at the base of Heideggerian philosophy. But
propositionalism, which denies interrogativity, is poorly equipped for
apprehending it without distorting the new reality which it aims at
conceptualizing. It brings it back to what existed, but from which it

nonetheless differs, and assigns it a minus sign: A and non-A. Everything and its opposite, thus the absurd. Deprived of all foundation, even our existence is absurd. We have no ultimate reason to do one thing instead of its opposite. But all discourse on existence is also absurd—an absurdity that has been reinforced by the two world wars which are the cause of Europe's decline. Everything in art—from literature to music— carries this idea of the lost identity of the stable and indubitable point of departure: the source of values, meaning, and ethics. The hidden order of art (to take up the title of Anton Ehrenzweig's book) is a chaos which is organized and mastered thanks to a greater abstraction and figuration. It is the image of the modern world, which has seen the ancient one collapse and fragmentation creep in where continuity once reigned. Our Peloponnesian wars will have led us to the same abyss: there was once Rome as there is now America. Literature, music, and painting, to name only these, have expressed that death of the subject.

The subject plays an essential role in literature: it gives to the narrative its unity—a sense, a direction which ties a beginning to an end; it totalizes a narration, it is the *for whom* and the *to whom* of the text. Once deprived of this fundamental role, subjects differ chapter after chapter. We see privileged points of view disappear and characters abound in epics that aim at reconstituting lost unity, as in James Joyce's *Ulysses* or today's South American novels. Meaning will henceforth be a problem, since there is no overarching subject for the narrative. The narrative thus fragments, becoming more abstract and enigmatic in relation to a real which conserves, in spite of it all, a certain stability, since *we*—each and every one of us—are its subject. But the subject that I am is also my neighbor, and the *I,* by dint of being everyone, is no longer but a "man without qualities," a quotidian Ulysses whose only adventure is everyone's nonadventure, an aseptized and organized universe, more anonymous than ever. It is at this stage that literary criticism joins the Marxist criticism of the dehumanized and atomized world which mechanizes the subject. Work, once liberating for the protestantism of the individual entrepreneur, becomes enslaving, once again, when the enterprise grows and becomes capitalized and hierarchical by means of the factory.

Through increased abstraction and the loss of stable and unique meaning, fiction, as in the *nouveau roman,* becomes nonstory and becomes more and more problematized. In this, it reflects a relationship to the real which is perceived more and more problematically, thus throwing into question the possibility of apprehending it as such. The very resources of discourse undergo the ordeal. The language of fiction changes into the object of fiction because the rhetoric of the real asserts itself as rhetoric. It is a matter of maintaining the identity of the real through all oppositions that signify difference, change, and nonidentity. A nonidentity which is thought (of) rhetorically is taken care of nonetheless, since that difference is thought of as rhetorical: rhetoric expresses what is nonidentical by presenting it metaphorically as identity. Rhetoric maintains the identity of the real by virtue of fiction. The work of art in general—aesthetics—could well be a response to the need to cultivate a rhetorical relationship with reality in order, precisely, to preserve its meaning as externalized and identical. By its rhetorical structure, the ego fulfills this role, even when it is a producer and consumer of ideology.

The problematization that was to affect discourse reflexively, without yet being able to understand itself as such, was to have as its effect the opening of modern culture to a plurality of meanings. Shattered identity must reestablish itself rhetorically, that is, as I have suggested, by the work of art, by form and by symbolization. Through the rhetoricization of the real (which grows quite generally so that reality in its very nature is maintained), the rhetorical component will assert and reveal itself in its role. The real which presents itself as rhetorical product discloses its imaginary and fictive unity, which only the symbolic allows us to apprehend. Here is indeed an image which suits a broken real. But the closure of *logos*—finally representing what it is, unable to continue repressing itself in a putative opening which would ensure, as if by magic, the eternal continuity of the world—this identity of the world detaches itself from reality in order that it be instituted on the rhetorical level as a figurative identity. Reality is restored. This discrepancy, or difference, becomes the literality of the *logos* that states the real, which is the same thing as the impossibility of stating the real in its own essential unity—in its evident unity. Literality is then itself the fiction of this *logos*. One cannot express things as they are without invoking what they are not. Heidegger very rightly stated this, thus bearing witness to the concern of maintaining a certain *logos*—be it poetic, but never interrogative, and reflexively so—allowing man to grant himself a sense of the lost identity elsewhere. The world according to *Being and Time* is made up of sign referrals, directions for use which solidify as soon as they point out things. Identity as image, as figure, as sign, as fiction with respect to a real identity (therefore unconscious of being an identity) is still reality in its irreducible form—with, as its keystone, a rhetoric whose forgetting is finally forgotten [*dont l'oubli est enfin oublié*] but whose interrogative nature remains unthinkable. The literal nonidentity of the world would be dreadful if it could not be reestablished at another level. And the price to be paid is this level of rhetoricization which the entirety of twentieth-century thought—from Heidegger to Perelman—has circumscribed in a multiplicity of ways. The breakage of the world, its fragmentation, is thinkable thanks to this: the meaning we can see in the loss of meaning will constitute its explication in the discourse that expresses *the* real as *broken.* Contradiction? No, metaphor—the supersession of fragmentation in its articulation. We of course know that when a Joyce, for example, speaks of everyday existence like a mythical epic, he immediately raises the question of whether it is so because he considers it impossible or if, on the contrary, he demands that we see life for what it is: a heroic adventure for each of us, but banal for everyone else. It is a bit like the cinematographer who films scenes of violence which we cannot decide whether he is condemning or praising. To speak is indeed to evoke a question, an alternative, by means of the answer which alone is delivered to us. "Under the short story and the chronicle, behind the blurry or brutal visions which form an unfinished whole, something of a mystery which remains an enigma imposes itself whose secret must not be provided by the organizer of these estrangements [*étrangements*]: at the same time as the novel becomes a difficult reality, it becomes a myth."[3] Here, the unified and coherent expression of the fragmentary along with the reflection of this discourse on itself is the proof of this rhetorical and mythical reestablishment of the whole.

Abstract art is thus the most realistic art there is: it makes sense of the nonsense by giving it a form, an appearance. The unity of gestalten is displaced outside the literality of works, therefore outside of that to which they refer. One must *search* and search elsewhere. This is what a symbolic system, which signifies literally nothing, forces us to do. Discontinuity results from the fragmentation of the literal and the figurative into a quest which is split off from the unity by rhetoric. "Discontinuity summons the notion of a world whose order is either absent or invisible," writes Ralph Heyndels in *La Pensée fragmentée*[4]—an alternative, a problem which may be summed up in the fact that a gestalt is literally asked as the rhetorical and subjacent figure behind this discontinuity. The entirety of art becomes enigmatic by allowing itself to be apprehended as rhetorical or formal: what it represents (because it is represented) is not expressed but suggested, evoked, dispersed in a whole that literality can only announce.

From the expressed, we move to the expression. The subject will be found everywhere—in the intentionality of language acts as well as in rhetoric in the broad sense—because, no longer "pure" as in Kant, subjectivity can finally be empirical, thus circumscribable. But subjectivity, which associates subjectively and sometimes with arbitrariness, is to be found especially in the receiver of works which no longer can have decipherable interpretations without an active intervention on his part. A hermeneutic act always results when something in the work abruptly confronts the receiver with the necessity of an interpretive demand. This receiver, reader, or listener must answer concerning the unity or the gestalt of the work of which he has become the depositary. The whole so-called school of reception (Hans Robert Jauss, Wolfgang Iser) has shown this, but by emphasizing one aspect which should be, nevertheless, correlated with deconstruction (Derrida), which has tried to show how all works deconstruct their unity by moving all the literal of its expression toward the impossibility of expressing itself as work. The text is thus a plurality of intertexts. Deconstructivism loses sight of the receiver's role and reception loses sight of the reflexivity of rhetoric that finally expresses and signifies itself at the outcome of its autonomization. But the process at the base is the same: radical problematization which both removes us from the real and puts us back into question in the evidence of what we are with respect to the world and, by this questioning, refers us to a multiplicity of possibilities. These possibilities, being enigmatic as they express literally something other than what they express, demand answers from those to whom they are intended: the audience. The work questions us even more, presents more of a problem, because it refers more to its problematicity, because it has rhetoric as its theme. "The novel itself, in its most recent forms, no longer attempts to represent a reality outside the work, but rather to lay bare the powers of writing as an operation upon language."[5]

Because of this very fact, enigmaticity arises (it is indissoluble from the deconstruction of every answer about the meaning of the text), leaving us with problematicity alone.

The combination of these complementary aspects has become a fact in fiction itself, but not in theory, which is still behind the times. Italo Calvino, for example, in his novel *If on a Winter Night a Traveller,* presents a narration which is built on the introduction of the reader, which disorients, breaks, and reorients the story. The book in the book and the reader in the book blend together. Moreover, Kafka already in the famous text of *Parables* brings to light the arising of rhetoric and what it implies for the apprehension of the signified.

"Were you to conform to symbols you would yourself become symbol and thus liberate yourself from your daily woes. Another might say: I wager that there's a symbol in that, too. The first responds: you would win. The second says: Yes, but sadly only symbolically. The first: No. In reality. For symbolically, you have lost."

Similarly, in *Die Prüfung* (*The Test*) we encounter the allegory of all literary modernity: the servant who gets hired because he cannot answer (because he does not even understand) the employer's questions. It is of course the reader—the servant of literature—who can no longer pose the question about meaning and find an answer outside of this question. By understanding that the answer is the question itself, he passes his test as reader. He has understood that what was to be understood was problematicity itself as the one and only answer. But without a problematology that can express the problematic without reabsorbing it into the assertorial which abolishes it, the servant's answer is absurd and comprehension falls back on unavoidable incomprehension.

Generally, the problematization of the subject is also equivalent to that of the reader, the spectator, and the listener. The literal, the appearance, that which shows itself the most directly, leads us to proceed further, demanding an interpretation because enigmaticity is this demand. The figurative of the literal is the articulation of a question and of an answer. Identity is the figurative: a question which is expressed in the fact of saying and which, for that reason, is never said (literally). *Gestalten* are no longer constituted but rather to be constituted. He who receives the artistic message knows full well that it is, as the term goes, "auto-referential" and that the gap it produces in relation to our references is meant to put us back into question. Thus the receiver becomes the producer of meaning—even of textuality—because he will have to structure it in its subjacent unity, which is figured in and by the text. Because the work responds by questioning (questioning its own meaning) and because the nature of a question is to refer to several possibilities for answering, the plurality of interpretations follows in entirely legitimate fashion. One could even say that if the meaning—in its unicity—still makes sense as a notion for the subject who receives the work, it is as question. Meaning as question is the answer to the question of the meaning insofar as the text always solicits its reader by a figurative demand. The content (thus the answer) varies: an answer which is all the more figurative because the text is literally enigmatic. The reader, the listener, the spectator are the respondents, just as an audience responds by agreement or disagreement.

3. FROM PROPOSITIONALIST IRRATIONALISM TO PROBLEMATOLOGICAL RATIONALITY

At the dawn of the twentieth century, Western reason was shaken in its most solid foundations. In the final analysis, Descartes had given it the grounding that Aristotle had failed to find. Cartesian thought was nevertheless to repeat the circularity of the Aristotelian foundation. Reason could make reason of everything except of the fact that it must make reason of everything. What was to become of rationality once its initial weakness was perceived? It would become increasingly technical: since global rationality is impossible, there only remain partial and analytic rationalities adapted to limited ends, even though these are often very complex. Adaptation to these ends was to be the byword of this Western rationality, impregnated as it was with the paradox of its existence beyond its successes. For although analytic reason may well be efficient (since it is centered on discrete and circumscribed objectives), it is no less paradoxical in its very foundation. For the very reason that it is partial, partial rationality which expresses Western rationality is no longer capable of calling it Reason at large. It nevertheless imposes itself as *the* rationality which prevails universally. Through the impossibility of being *the* rationality, partial rationalities are globally irrational. We have a model of rationality which is entirely fragmented and pragmatic and which, through its universalization, is credited with something that it cannot be. How could a reason which is no more than partial become accepted as global without there being contradiction? Science and technology merge here at the heart of this analytic reason which is both impossible and terribly efficient: impossible as model and practical as directions for use. Reason collapses, a certain humanism disappears. We have moved from the man-subject to the man-object, along with all the disastrous moral consequences which derive from it. Analytic reason is theoretical, and cynical or instrumental reason is practical.

Is it, as some claim, a legacy of positivism from the beginning of the century? From the moment that discourse can only gloss endlessly upon the impossibility of all discourse, discursivity, through the reflection of its own fundamental problematicity, escapes its former coherence for want of problematological discourse. Not only can it no longer be resolved, but it cannot be expressed. The propositional model is indifferent to this move from the answer to the problematic. The silence in the last aphorism in Wittgenstein's *Tractatus,* like that associated with Being through the silent and attentive listening that it demands, according to Heidegger, points to the horizon. Thought, deprived of the possibility of resolving the questions it poses, must answer this challenge by proclaiming the impossibility of answering. This is nihilism.

The other path has consisted in taking science as the resolutive model. Science resolves all questions without necessitating an anthropological foundation. This is positivism. Philosophy must not only study science but also become science. If nihilism is contradictory in the very terms by which it must be formulated, logical empiricism—which is neither empirically founded nor logically valid—bears testimony to an identical self-defeating discourse. These two moments could not survive as such. But responding to an insurmountable crisis of propositional rationality, they displaced themselves in other forms while maintaining, nevertheless, their own "principles."

The two reactions to the radical problematization of Western thought proceed from a process perpetuated in contemporary reflection— always with the same blinding. The death of the subject—which closely follows the death of God, as we know—is not conceived of in terms of problematization, since only propositionalism is available. Propositionalism knows neither answer nor question but only the proposition, even when it questions or answers, which are two modalities distinguishable for it only by the psychological and intellectual activity which is implemented in it. For nihilism, answering has become impossible, while for positivism only science possesses efficacy in answering. These two conceptions will face off throughout the century. But what must be noted is that the fate always reserved for propositional *logos* continues to be decided on its own basis, without our feeling obliged to conceptualize the interrogativity of the *logos,* thus to radically change what Western tradition has conceived as *logos.* Problematization is not apprehended in itself but rather through the propositionalist prism along with the correlative question: Can we still put forth propositions? Some answer no; others answer yes, by accepting efficacity, technical operatory, and analytic and scientific reason. This very vision of what answering means has not been put into question in itself. This conception results from the disappearance of the preexisting framework and of the limited headlong flight which a science with ungeneralizable mechanisms offers up very reassuringly (in that its operationality rests on partial and concentrated areas of the realms of masterable objects). All of this perhaps explains why the thought that issued from nihilism has hardly advanced any more than that born of analytic reason and logical empiricism. The fact that man ceases being what he was and institutes himself in a discrepancy with himself, in the nonidentity with self, appears in different forms in structuralism, with Foucault, Derrida, Lacan, and even Sartre. When he speaks of the for-itself as being that which it is not and as not being what it is, with "bad faith" as this very alterity in the tissue of consciousness, it is difficult to identify consciousness in its traditional Cartesian texture. We could expound on the flight into history and into literature in order to face the impossibility of maintaining a nonabsurd discourse upon the absurdity of existence. Western reason, Foucault says, owes its putative universality solely to the exclusion of all transgression: madness, the prison, and sexuality each illustrate the cracks in this rationality, which universalizes at little cost without being able to explain, or at least which remains silent about what constitutes its margins. These areas, which classical reason was unable to integrate, should give birth to a new anthropology. The discrepancy with self in time is already to be found in Heidegger, where the accent is on temporality which reestablishes non-identity without contradiction. But it is principally with Derrida and Lacan that this discrepancy can be discerned the best. With Derrida, it is *différance,* but above all absent presence (A and non-A); with Lacan, it is desire without saturation, thus an unconscious semiotized by the discrepancy without any identity possible of the signifier and of that to which it refers.

It could have therefore been hoped that the death of the subject as the death of the out-of-the-question which decides beforehand about all possible resolutions (making questioning rhetorical and propositionally redundant with respect to the assertability of the subject by itself) would, by undermining this assertability, open the way for a problematology, thus for a nonpropositional rhetoric in which the *a priori* would cease to be rediscovered. What is found, according to propositionalism, is determined *a priori.* After all, if the out-of-the-question (the human subject in question) problematizes itself, and becomes in turn the subject of an alternative (A and non-A), one might hope that the foundation (with the help of problematization) would allow the latter to express itself in its very fundamentality. Nothing of the sort took place. The alternative and the alternative couples have been integrated into more or less classical relationships (such as A/A, B/B, etc.) which structuralism, from Claude Lévi-Strauss to A. J. Greimas, has delighted in [*être friand*] without really going beyond. However, the fact that man happens to be in question by ceasing to be out-of-the-question (which coincided with his general study and his multiple expression at numerous levels) should have alerted us to the presuppositions of the binary mechanism [*de couplage*]. Indeed, far from constituting an "epistemo-

logical break," the semioticization of human reality is part of a continuous evolutionary mechanism of inference whose problematological nature can no longer be doubted. What does it mean to infer? Aristotle
expressed it well: produce a discourse from something other than what
was supposed at the outset (*Prior Analytics,* I, 1, 24b18–22). Without
such a difference between conclusion and point of departure, there is no
inference. For if the conclusion, which is offered as the resolution of a
question, is contained in the out-of-the-question, it cannot really be
maintained that anything whatsoever has been resolved. The essential
difference to be respected, so that in the final analysis there is a *logos,* is
what I call the problematological *difference* which demarcates questions
from answers. It is the necessary and sufficient condition for there to be
a solution and knowledge of the solution. For Aristotle, the vicious circle
is a simple propositional matter, a link between propositions, a link
which is not explained except, precisely, in circular fashion. Or, through
the opposition of the known and the unknown, it is psychological: by
moving in circles, one does not progress. And at the same time it is
necessary (as John Stuart Mill would say against Aristotle's logic in the
name of those very principles) that the conclusion be "contained" in the
premises. In reality, the difference between the out-of-the-question and
the question helps to establish the answer, and it is truly in problematological terms that the inferential discourse finds the justification
of its validity, of its fecundity, and, consequently, of its existence. Moreover, like any discourse, the inference answers a question one has in
mind, a question which is brought up by what one says as well as by the
fact that one says it.

But as soon as it was born, deduction lost the sense of its origins. As an
establishing of problematological difference, it is nevertheless nothing
more than the resolution of one question mediated through another to
which there is already an answer. Put in very general terms, the answer is
arrived at through a question of which it is not the solution. Otherwise,
we would of course have a circle. We will have B rather than non-B
because we have A (rather than non-A) at the beginning. This is the
model of causal argument: With the out-of-the-question A, can one make
a decision on the question B? If A is the subject and it is in question in
turn, there is an A/non-A, B/non-B relationship. A signifying B is at best an
indication for concluding B, but nothing excludes the possibility that
non-A be associated with B (or with non-B) as well. All of this has
become problematical, but it will not be said: rather, we will prefer to
specify that A is the sign of B and that A and B have a relation of
significance between them. This is the sole propositionalist manner of

facing the loss of constraint. To speak regarding man of signifier and signified allows us to grasp that man can be other (A and non-A) and that, at the most, we can detect signs of what he is and no longer describe him with the unshakable Cartesian certainty of yesterday (i.e., exclude one of the possibilities, A or non-A). An inference, however, has never been more than a question that is resolved on the basis of another one, thus an answer that serves to resolve a question other than the one to which it refers directly. The doubling of the literal and the figurative indeed constitutes an inference dependent on the reader. Rhetoric and argumentation merge in the underlying problematological mechanism which makes of each of them an inference.

Man, who in structuralism works his way into the gap opened between signifiers and signified, is thus the sign of his inadequacy to himself—his truth and nontruth. This means that he is problematized by problematization (the signifier) of the real (the signified), i.e., that the two no longer adhere but arbitrarily, as Ferdinand de Saussure might have said. By this characterization, man is put into an alternative: he was A; now, because he is no longer the indisputable subject he was before, he can be non-A. He is rhetoricized. But for us this means, at a deeper level, that he is problematized. Rhetoricization is indeed that which prepares his problematological conceptualization. For it is important to grasp that the birth of man, like his death, only constitutes a breakage by virtue of the very terms that are put to use. What could be more disruptive than a beginning or an end? But all of this takes place on a canvas of negation of questioning. By introducing strict causality, the classical mechanism needed man or even God as a support/mainstay. When this causality disappears (among other reasons because it is incapable of covering the entire modern and contemporary explanatory field), man-foundation disappears in the wake of God's disappearance. Inference becomes flexible to the point that it ends up reflexively integrating the initial problematization upon which it rests. Failing to refer to types of problematics which inference resolves differently for different historical periods, it will appear to us that there are successive moments considered autonomous, distinct, fragmentary, whereas they have a hand in the laws of questioning as these unfold historically. Man-foundation no longer has a *raison d'être* when rationality becomes rhetoricized. This is a result of a greater problematization. The closing of *logos* then passes through the thematization of the field of argumentation. This closure thus becomes a rhetoric of reason, an ideologization which says itself [*qui se dit*].

Closure may then be perceived as unmasked on the individual (psychoanalytic) as well as on the collective (Marxist) level. But in so doing, these "new rhetorics" reveal themselves immediately for what they are: guarantors of the closure of propositional *logos*. These guarantors are themselves closed rhetorically, which is something that Karl Popper denounced with regard to psychoanalysis and the ideological analysis of ideology, that is, Marxism. The function of the rhetoricization of *logos* is to preserve the resolutive automatism of the latter. This in turn maintains the sophistic role of rhetoric, which allows it to reduce any question to an "already there" answer. The fracture caused by the radical problematization of the last century is thus swallowed up in a purely rhetorical nonidentity. It is perhaps to this phenomenon that we owe the survival of propositional *logos*. In spite of this, such a *logos* cannot perpetuate itself, for a rhetoric which expresses itself as such may very well be also propositionalized (which circularizes the "solution"). Rhetoric nevertheless reveals the essential fracture from which this *logos* suffers. Unmasked closure can only make reason, in spite of its denials, take the alternative to *logos* that is expressed inside *logos* into account. This forces reason to change itself in order to think itself through alternatives (alternatives which would no longer be some proposition existing before all question); this is to say that it is important to be able to assume interrogativity as such from itself. Explaining, unveiling, and autonomizing itself, rhetoric appears to fictively restore identity and, at the same time, to rip *logos* from its heretofore inexpressible closure. This is an insoluble contradiction, for the breakage cannot simultaneously be said and denied constantly by this expression. This explains the illusory and precarious character of the rhetoricization of propositional *logos*, especially since this rhetoricization proceeds according to the same propositional order which leads questions back to preliminary assertions. Henceforth, the rhetoric which develops in this *logos* can only be auto-confirmed as propositional and not integrate the opposition, the alternative in what it implements in a problematic way. The rhetoric of propositional *logos* checks it at the very moment and place which put the *logos* into question while canceling it. Rhetoricizing *logos* can, in any case, dispense with the anthropological foundation born of mechanistic causality; it has been doing this since the beginning of the century. In order for the rationality of *logos* to survive this rhetoricization without perpetuating today's irrationalism, *logos* must become interrogative so that it can express its own problematization and, consequently, all other problematizations. What this rhetoricization shows is precisely the original flaw in propositional *logos*, with its closures revealing themselves for what they are: rhetorical illusions which are merely sophistic, an identity of purely fictive reason which gives our rationality over to the chaos of unreason under the pretense of being capable of assimilating everything. The identity of Western reason implies the abandonment of propositionalism, which has run its course in spite of its many avatars. On the other hand, remaining in an unchanged framework, we have no choice but to take note of the break—the breaks—which are, when all is said and done, nothing more than the problematological expressions of repressed historicity. If the anthropological moment is made absolute, outside a wider historical context, the end of this moment will be the end of reason. This is exactly what Foucault's epistemology of the break [*coupure*] implies. With the death of man-foundation disappears a form of [*la*] rationality, but not rationality at large, which changes appearance to allow man to not play the role of God any longer and to retrieve a perhaps more human location to redefine. If one considers the defundamentalization of the subject as an end, one can but fall into pure nihilism or positivist illusion.

4. FROM ANTHROPOLOGY TO ETHICS

The death of man, rigorously understood as the death of man-foundation, was to be nothing less than the announcement of the moral decline of the West, whose political aspects were to be concretized, at least in Europe, by the two world wars. From the moment one ceases to treat the Other as subject, the way to barbarianism is opened. Instrumentality in human relations has, of course, less terrible manifestations, but it is never but the consequence of the generalization of an exchange economy in which one gives only in order to receive and in which it is enough that taking advantage of the Other be rational. Valueless and idealless materialism has thus been able to implant itself in other cultures, like in Japan, without really upsetting existing values, to the extent that, with us, there was nothing which would have contradicted anything whatsoever. On the other hand, some societies—like certain Islamic cultures of today—which are both more fragile and more archaic in many respects, have preferred to reject the West. Perhaps the most appalling spectacle is that of our own dissolution and of a progression in cynicism with its cohort of sophists. Rhetorical awareness derives from a need for closure in broken *logos.* In this perspective, rhetoric swallows all opposition; it is assimilated into the sophistic by this function of automaticization of the resolutive. If, on the other hand, it is realized that rhetoric is in the service of insurmountable questions *per se,* automatism is broken and propositional *logos* gives way to a true conception of answering [*répondre*]. Sophistic thought is spineless [*molle*] and will fail to convince when it comes time to erect a rampart to protect the highest values, like the rights of man. Under these conditions, how will we defend the dignity of the human being, who is scoffed at in so many areas in the name of sacrifices imposed by History and its radiant future. Have we, in the end, nothing other than a hazy and empty thought (attended, it is true, by a thousand rhetorical devices) to set against historicism, which indeed appears to represent the last substantial anthropology? On the other hand, how is one to accept a conception of man which reduces him to a mere instrument at the service of a destiny which inevitably swallows him up? A rhetorical anthropology founds the right of the Other to throw any answer back into question. It not only gives him *eo ipso* the right to free expression, to difference, it also confers upon him the freedom to put it into practice. Because each of us is both the questioner and the respondent, the responsibility which compels us to justify ourselves in consideration of these fundamental rights proceeds from their very exercise. And because this practice is ours as well as that of the Other, the universality which respects his problematicity will ensue necessarily.

2

Rhetoric in the Twentieth Century:
From Proposition to the Question

1. RHETORIC AND THE INTELLECTUAL CRISIS OF OUR TIME

hen historians of thought char-
acterize the distinctive features of the twentieth century, the fact that
will impose itself is, I think, the foundational crisis which has shaken
Western culture at large. As Christine Brooke-Rose points out,

> that this century is undergoing a reality crisis has become a banal-
> ity, easily and pragmatically shrugged off. Perhaps it is in fact
> undergoing a crisis of the imagination; a fatigue, a decadence. And
> rhetoricians usually appear in times of decadence, that is, when
> stable values disappear, when forms break down and new ones
> appear, coexisting with all the old ones. Their task is then to try to
> make sense of what is happening by working out reasoned
> typologies of structures. . . . Today the rhetoricians of innumera-
> ble kinds are more voluble than they have been for centuries.[1]

The revival of rhetoric can be seen as one of the numerous manifestations of our nihilistic present. The loss of indisputable principles has

rendered nearly everything questionable, arguable. Hence the multiplicity of equally defensible values and opinions on many subjects, except in
science, which has benefited from such a crisis. Is scientific thought
really the last refuge of reason? In contrast, we shall have to ask ourselves
whether rhetoric amounts to a mere manipulative technique, a devalu-
ated mode of solving problems. This, in turn, evokes the old, and perhaps
more fundamental criticism leveled by Plato against rhetoric. In my eyes,
however, a certain conception of rhetoric, rooted in the question-view,
can provide an adequate response to the crisis. Before tackling this
question, and even in order to solve it, we must describe more fully the
crisis from which the revival of rhetorical thought has emerged in our
century. This description will also enable us to situate rhetoric in a wider
context and will even provide some clue in the search for a general
theoretical framework for rhetoric. The reason for this confidence does
not so much lie in some personal inclination toward the historical approach as in the idea that the *nature* of the crisis should be read *from*
history. And if we can understand the crisis as a cultural phenomenon
with its structural features, we shall also be able to move one step
further, since we shall be able to then deal with those structural characteristics alone. I do not intend to provide a structuralist approach to
rhetoric, however, but a reading *from* history. Such a reading will allow
me to go beyond the problems bequeathed by history and to address
them as problems, with a solution which does not accept them as inevitable, as factual, as historically *there* once and for all in their disruptive
legacy. History is a means to go beyond history; in this respect, I prefer to
say that my method rests upon *historicity*, because it is based on the
relation between what changes and what does not, in order to understand what has been (and which is always what has been *for us now*).
Once the problems have been discovered with the help of such a
method, they are dealt with according to their structural, internal, and
even autonomous distinctive features.

Rhetoric appears forcefully in times of crisis, as Brooke-Rose says, for
the simple reason that only the lack of directing principles in the settling
of questions causes these questions to be relentlessly submitted to controversial answers. In the absence of leading principles that could point
to some definitive, univocal, answer that would exclude any other, the
problem is bound to be disputed and solved "equivocally"; that is, with
an answer that is not unique and possible once and for all. What is the
ultimate principle of thought and action, of philosophy and moral conduct, which has collapsed, letting the other rules based on it collapse
little by little, one by one? Basically, we could say that the two world

wars have had the same effect upon the Western world as the Peloponnesian wars had on ancient Greece. In both cases, we observe a collapse of
previous and well-established values and modes of thought, with an
increased individualism which fosters recourse to rhetorical devices to
relate to others. And, in turn, to the theoretization of those devices: from
the Sophists to Aristotle, rhetoric underwent a codification that, in our
times, Perelman as well as others have restored. But this is merely a
description of a political crisis. We now know that the crisis has also an
economic counterpart, as witnessed by the successive waves of unem-
ployment and inflation that we have known throughout this century. The
crisis has also, if not most of all, deep intellectual aspects that are more
ancient and that define its specificity much more adequately. I am even
quite ready to say that the crisis we now know (and in the terms we
know it today, socially , politically, and economically) has its roots in the
foundational crisis that our culture at large underwent at the end of the
nineteenth century with Marx, Nietzsche, and Freud. The cultural aspects have accumulated and met the economic, social, and political
features. Together, they have brought the decay that had been an-
nounced a century ago by those who could not believe in rationality as it
had been theorized by Descartes and Kant. The economic, social, and
political disruptions of our century have shaken the model of reason that
our society has generalized at all its levels. The confirmation of the
failure of rationality as conceived since Descartes is all the more striking
in that it has served as a general model of reason. The death of the ego, of
the Cartesian ego, the ultimate foundation of knowledge and, since Kant,
of ethics and conduct, has in some way found its verification in the
emergence of the so-called *era of the masses.* Auschwitz and the atom
bomb have symbolized the destructive aspects of this overall rationality,
which has led to a vision of the absurd from which we have not really
departed yet. Rationality at its extreme has given way to irrationality and
absurdity. Reason as a whole seems unable to account for the whole,
hence for its own will to account for everything. Reason, thus, can
explain everything except its own will to explain everything. The death
of the Cartesian ego has separated philosophy, i.e., reason, from its ultimate foundation. The role played by the *cogito* was to provide a key to
any possible question that could arise. It was the condition of any possible answer, the criterion of answerhood at large. The *cogito* is therefore,
in Descartes's own terms, the unquestionable, indubitable, starting point
of all inquiry. If everything is called into question, that which remains
out-of-question is the questioner himself, the Self. The identity of the
questioner is maintained throughout all possible questions, i.e., indepen-

dently of the alternatives that present themselves. The Self is then the substance (that is, the subject) of any alternative, of any prob-lematization, without being itself other than what it is. This is why I can doubt anything, and an "Evil Genius" can induce any error in me, but never can I doubt that I doubt, therefore, that I am. A variation, an alternative way of conceiving a subject, is a predicate. The human sub-ject will then become the unquestionable subject underlying all possible question.

Kant extended the scope of subjectivity to the sphere of ethics, be-stowing thereby upon the *cogito* a generalized fundamentality that was implied in Descartes without being fully stated. The first answer affirmed as being the "I think," being the model of answerhood, serving as the measure of all future and possible answers, universalized subjectivity was to become the form of all moral norms.

With Marx, Nietzsche, and Freud—and we could include Kierkegaard as well in the list—the subject came under attack: it ceased to be out-of-the-question and was considered no longer as a foundation for knowl-edge and action. Is consciousness, transcendental or not, the unquestion-able ground for all that which is essentially human, ranging from history to science, from art to affective and sexual relationships? In fact, the unquestioned priority of consciousness was called into question when philosophers began to realize that the subject was governed by uncon-scious motives, that ethical justifications were quite often mere rational-izations borrowed from the ruling ideological structures, and that free-dom was a kind of subjective illusion with respect to the sociohistorical determinants of behavior. Hence the question arose as to the grounding capacity of the subject defined as consciousness. The subject then ap-peared more as a result than a beginning, i.e., as the foundation of all possible results. Emerging from the interplay of quite a number of forces, subjective as much as historical, over which consciousness has no power, the ego of the *cogito* ceased to be the condition of possibility that it had been since Descartes and Kant.

And the deconstruction of the subject began. The subject lost little by little its unquestionable status. This, as Foucault has shown in *The Order of Things,* coincided with the birth of the human and social sciences. Man could be studied like any other object, since the subject had no longer a privileged ontological status with respect to the other aspects of reality. The nineteeth century thus saw the birth of the *Geisteswissen-schaften* at the same time as the "defundamentalization" of thought and even of Western culture at large. Literature reflected the same evolution with the abandonment of the privileged standpoint in narratives. The implied narrator, as being the "subject" of the story, once marked the beginning and the end of the narrative, which thereby made sense, a meaning defined in reference to him as the source of significance of the progressive unfolding. The very notion of a narrative as a totality, with a beginning and an end, referring to a given subject who embraces them and ascribes them a meaning from his point of view on the whole, ceased to prevail. This absent, implied subject of fiction vanished little by little from the literary landscape, as attested by, for example, Virginia Woolf's novels or the *nouveau roman.* "It is true that in Virginia Woolf's novels, as in a great deal of modern fiction, the narrator's personality is effaced, her role as commentator, greatly reduced."[2] The absence of an implied narrator for whom the story progresses will evidently bring about the absence of any progression in the narrative, which will then become more and more enigmatic. A basic rhetorical feature of this problematicity is the breaking down of the linearity of time. Time is experienced as unquestionable when its order is progressive. What does *progressive* mean here? Problems receive a solution, and the latter comes naturally *after* the former. One only pays attention to time when progressiveness breaks down; this, in turn, implies that problems remain without solution, or that their solution *continues* to evoke the problems it was meant to solve. The linear order of a narrative is disrupted by time-ruptures, and the story cannot but draw our attention to its own problematicity through its being unresolved. This is, of course, one textual arrangement, i.e., one rhetorical device, among others that bring problematicity to the fore.

The breaking down of forms, as we find it in poetry, is another constitutive characteristic of the rhetoric of problematicity, a rhetoric which defines the modernity of contemporary rhetoric. Poetry, as noted before, will follow the movement by rendering its forms more and more enigmatic as to *what* is said, as well as for *whom* and by *whom* it is said. Since the phenomenon is a general one, no wonder that we also find it in painting and in music.

> In serialization, the same elements are scrambled up in every possible sequence so that their relationship becomes quite obscure to conscious hearing. Yet the composer insists, that contrary to appearances all variations are somehow equivalent. . . . Yet Schoenberg considered this back-to-front reversal as the most characteristic variation of his theme. For him the twelve tones of the chromatic scale were the eternal theme containing from the outset the ulimited number of permutations which are supposed

to preserve intact the identity of the theme. We are once again confronted with the chaos of the primary process which treats temporal and spatial cohesion with the same cavalier contempt. The identity of temporal sequence as the principle of an acoustic Gestalt is paralleled in vision by the identity of spatial distribution. It is difficult to recognize an object if it is shown upside down, almost impossible if the spatial relationships between its elements are scrambled up. But this is precisely what happens in Picasso's portraits and in his arbitrary conglomerations of the human figure.[3]

This text is important in more than one respect. It draws attention to the relationship between the role of identity, the ego, and modern art in general. Serialization is the musical mode of fragmentation, which is a general, if not constitutive, characteristic of the unconscious. Our epoch, because of such effects, could not but discover the unconscious. The established structures of identity that define the Self cannot repeat themselves and perpetuate their own stability. Difference has to come up as the expression of the problematicity of these very structures. But problematicity will not be conceptualized as such; only difference within structures will be. This will be *structuralism,* as we now know it through Foucault, Derrida, Lévi-Strauss, and Lacan. I can only but agree with John Fekete, when he writes in his remarkable introduction to *The Structural Allegory:*

> What is at stake in the encounter with the structural turn is the Western mind itself.... The strategic move effected in the language paradigm is the refusal of conscious, intentional sources of meaning.... The structural allegory renders problematical all the (ultimately) self-betraying affirmations of the effective subjectivity of the human individual or the progress of history.... The structural allegory constructs the place of the individual only negatively, as an absent otherness, a faded tract in the problematization of the human.[4]

We now understand the importance of Saussure for the whole movement. His system functions as a structure because the internal variations or differences within the system constitute its identity and, in turn, give meaning to each individual item, as an individual, within the system. *Difference* is the key word here: it is otherness in the system which brings about the identity of the elements. History, as much as the human subject, can be codified within this structural framework, since change is a difference with respect to what was before. These differences are internal to the system itself, which can then capture them and not only be submitted to them externally. As to the human Self, it is always something *other*—a mirror, a dialectic of identifications. Sartre used to call it transcendence, but with structuralism and under Saussure's influence the Self came to be described as a sign, a trace, whose identity is precisely to refer to something other than itself. When the Self tries to proceed otherwise, through reflection, for instance, it will feel the distance between the signifier and the signified (Lacan), which means that the gap is eternally unbridgeable. Hence, the Self is a mere trace (Derrida) of a process of infinite and impossible catching up (*différance*). Man will therefore inhabit the "arbitrariness of the sign," as Saussure is supposed to have put it (though with another idea in mind). The arbitrariness of the sign is actually the space in which man exists as such. If there were a natural adequacy between man and reality, the signifier and the signified would be undifferentiated. But the signifier only denotes a given signified arbitrarily, for conventional or pragmatic purposes. What is meant is not naturally so, but only intentionally or in virtue of the laws of a given system. The distance between man and what he is not is measured as a difference, the repetition of the inadequacy of the signifier to the signified. The signifier of my Self will be the product of an unconscious displacement historically and individually conditioned, of a reality, i.e., my Self, which cannot be but metaphorically, allegorically, apprehended. Once again, as in poetry and literature at large, form becomes more and more assimilated to metaphors. The identity of the Self, ensured by the transparency of consciousness through its own reflexivity, will disappear, to become a metaphorical identity, i.e., something which is itself by being something other, a displacement of something which is bound to remain unidentical with oneself in the strict acceptation of the term *identity,* due to the role played by the unconscious.

The Self has become a question, an enigma, and literature will express this historical fact with another much favored procedure, the problematization of its own possibility. Hence, "the self is not named in these works largely because it is extralinguistic. What is named is the problem of naming. One connection among these books, then, is that each attempts to do the impossible."[5] Literature, in the twentieth century, has increasingly become a deconstruction of the ego, a formalization of its own impossibility to constitute itself, due to the impossibility of maintaining a privileged standpoint, as it used to be.

The same situation can be found in poetry.

Eliot's new mode of characterization derives from the romantic attempt to deal with the increasingly problematic nature of the self. Eliot's nameless, faceless voices express the sense—which by the twentieth century has come to prevail—that the self, if it exists at all, is changing and discontinuous and that its unity is as problematic as its freedom from external conditions.[6]

The increased anonymity, i.e., depersonalization, that we find in modern narratives ("who speaks"?), embodied in Joyce's *Ulysses* or Robert Musil's *Man without Qualities,* finds its natural consequence in the literary question of literary thematization, thereby rendering the logic of modern writing more auto-referential than ever. Fiction has become metafictional. It came to express problematicity more and more, through enigmatic modes of writing. This questioning refers back to the question of the Self, or the Self as question. Traditionally, the Self, or the I, has been conceived of as the unity of experience, that which synthesizes the diversity of sensations into a homogenous reality. The fragmentation of reality refers back to the correlative fragmentation of the Self as a pole of unification. The puzzle of existence mirrors the increased absurdity of the real as being a discontinuous bundle of experiences. The Self reflects the question that the whole is now for himself, including himself as a mere part of it.

One example can illustrate my argument. I return to a text written by Kafka in 1920, *Die Prüfung* (*The Test*). Here, the author depicts a character who wants to become a servant but fails to get hired. On one evening, he meets an important servant of the house at a tavern.

> "Why do you want to run away? Sit down and have a drink! I'll pay." So I sat down. He asked me several things, but I could not answer, indeed I didn't even understand his questions. So I said: "Perhaps you are sorry now that you have invited me, so I'd better go," and I was about to get up. But he stretched his hand out over the table and pressed me down. "Stay," he said, "that was only a test. He who does not answer the questions has passed the test."[7]

At first reading, we are tempted to say that what is going on in this story is merely absurd. Who will ever get hired by not answering the questions of the examiner? Let us call this reading the traditional one: Kafka is the painter of the absurd. This interpretation, however, is hardly receivable, even if it turns out to be the easiest one to profess. But, why would Kafka say anything if nothing can be said?

A second line of interpretation, called deconstructivism, will be structuralist in spirit in the sense that it will consider the text as a code for
textuality itself, a secret language referring to language itself, a signifier
indirectly signifying itself through its very semiological function. In
Kafka's example, such an interpretation would lead to the following
reading: The servant who cannot enter the house is like the reader who
cannot understand modern literature. Any text evokes the question of its
meaning to the reader—the "servant" of the text—but the reader will
only have access to the meaning of modern fiction if he understands that
there is no longer a meaning to find. He will pass the test of the reader,
like the servant in Kafka's narrative, if he realizes that the question itself
is meaningless. As a result, he will obtain the only possible answer and he
will have access to the text.

The deconstructivist will merely say that we here have a text referring
to literature itself, that we have an allegory of fiction by fiction. He will
probably also affirm that this text bears more specifically on the meaninglessness of the question of meaning and that the only meaning of textuality so conceived is that it has no meaning. This apparent paradox resolves itself fictionally.

I shall not deny this interpretation which I have myself brought to
light,[8] playing, as it were, the devil's advocate. My claim is that such an
interpretation is a denial of any possible interpretation and that it, therefore, defeats itself, because it nonetheless serves as an interpretation. In
other words, the deconstructivist reading, here, gives the impression,
but only an impression, of going beyond the mere constative statement
of absurdity.

Contradiction, however, can be avoided. The question of meaning, if
we accept that it is allegorically raised in Kafka's text, does not lead to
the meaninglessness of the text but to the idea of meaning as a question
posed by the text itself. Meaning is still an answer, but, in modern fiction,
an answer on the questionable. The question of meaning has to remain
without answer, but this is already an answer. In fact, the answer is the
question itself: the meaning of fictional texts now imposes itself as the
affirmation of their problematicity.

Problematicity is the key word. It expresses the overall tragedy of
culture in the twentieth century, a tragedy which is experienced as a
crisis of principles. Everything can now be called into question, and
Kafka illustrates this fact as much as any other major contemporary
writer. Philosophy will not be spared, either. Here, too, problematicity
will not, and could not, be conceptualized for itself. This is why it will be
seen as something exclusively negative. Philosophy is undermined in its

foundation. As a result, it will reflect problematization because of its incapacity to solve its own problems. The problematization of philosophy by itself led to a crisis of confidence in its own discourse. Such a situation of internal doubt without an undoubted solving principle could only reflect itself in two ways. The first one I have called *negative metaphysics,* or *nihilism,* and the other is better known under the label of *neopositivism,* or *logical empiricism.*

Let us first see why and how nihilism has molded the landscape of contemporary thought. Problematization has become the very problem of philosophy because there is no guarantee any more that a true solution has been found. Deprived of its traditional and unquestionable principle for dealing with its problems, philosophy has become a problem for itself, the problem of its own possibility as a solving-process. This is an unsolvable problem, for the simple reason that this problem states the impossibility of its being answered. Nihilism accepts this Heideggerian *Holzweg,* and even proclaims that what is essential cannot be said any longer. With Heidegger and Wittgenstein, who also upholds a negative metaphysics, if not a fascination with nihilism as defined above, the theme of silence will become prominent. Philosophy, being now impossible, can only say that it cannot say anything. Outside the affirmation of its own impossibility, philosophy, unless trivialized, must remain silent or attempt another way of dealing with problems. Silence, then, is really the only solution left to be *said.* "The highest thinking saying rests in this, not simply to keep silent what is authentically to be said in that saying, but to say it in such a way that it is named in the not-speaking: the saying of thinking is a silencing."[9] As to Wittgenstein's last aphorism in the *Tractatus,* it is too well known to be cited again, but here too we have a similar profession of silence.

The above position is, of course, untenable because it is contradictory in principle. How could discursivity establish its validity on its own ruins? How is it possible, for a given discourse, to affirm that it cannot speak any more; how could we even say that *nothing* can be said anymore? This situation may have led several thinkers to go to sources outside philosophy. Some have looked to literature (Jean-Paul Sartre, Albert Camus) for the solution to the generalization of absurdity (generalization, because it extended from discourse to existence and, consequently, to the discourse on existence), or, more radically, as in the case of Heidegger, to a new mode of speech, such as poetry.

The avowal of the impossibility to hold any philosophical discourse as being the only remaining philosophical possibility to affirm anything is, properly speaking, nihilistic. This attitude was bound to lead its advocates to the rejection of science as an illusory solution, since such a solution would imply that science is *the* only remaining or possible criterion of assertability. But efficiency does not prove the presence of the impossible principle. Science is a false ontology, a metaphysics which does not question its own principles and which structurally *cannot* even question them. This is why science can do without an *a priori* explication of its ultimate ground (*pace* Descartes), and, moreover, must do without asking such a question. Metaphysics truly understood, on the contrary, should raise the problem of its own solving procedures, if any, and not merely apply them. It is in the very nature of philosophy to display and render explicit the historical and intellectual presuppositions of its problematization (Heidegger). And to show, thereby, why and how philosophy has come to an end, after Hegel, with Nietzsche. Philosophy is now unable to treat the questions it usually posed and to say anything about them, unless it is to render explicit how such a situation has been brought about. *Negative metaphysics* tells us why philosophy is impossible and what it cannot claim anymore: its sole positivity resides in highlighting its own fate. If philosophical discourse cannot be pursued, science, as a substitute, is a deceit in this respect, and for the very same reason.

In spite of this radical rejection of science, many philosophers have put all their hopes in science as the only means to save philosophy from its own despair and self-destruction. After all, science solves the questions that it raises. Is this not a good reason to study science, to adopt the method of science in philosophy, and, therefore, to transform philosophy into a scientific enterprise? Science, obviously, has not undergone a *general* crisis of problematization, but only local ones, and this should suggest that its procedure and methodology are more adequate.

What is then a real question? A question that can be solved and eliminated thereafter. All those that cannot be solved are not real questions. This view of reasoning rests upon the idea that the meaning of a question is its solution (Moritz Schlick, Rudolf Carnap), because nobody would really ask a question if he did not want and hope to get an answer. Who, then, would raise a question that is structurally, i.e., logically, without solution? A question means a real problem if it has a solution, and the solution suppresses what is problematic. The question disappears once it is solved, as in science; when questions do not disappear, as in metaphysics, they do not express real problems. Logic, thus, is a mode of univocal resolution, as well as experience. If I ask whether John came yesterday, experience will tell me univocally whether he came or not. *Logical empiricism* was, quite naturally, the label attached to this view. Philosophy, facing the internal crisis of solving its problems, borrowed a problem-solving attitude which was deemed able to overcome the crisis. Problematicity had to disappear by the adoption of a model that makes problems disappear, i.e., solve them or dissolve them.

This has been the second way, and could be the only alternative for survival. This one has been opposed to metaphysics as much as metaphysics has been opposed to logical positivism. Each had a different view on questioning and answerhood, even though neither really bothered to ground it in a thorough analysis of questioning itself. It was sufficiently evident, for positivism, that answers give the meaning of the questions they suppress once these questions have been solved. Efficiency seemed to be the unquestionable assumption to be made. But here, too, the position rapidly proved untenable. The criterion of meaningfulness could not justify its own meaningfulness, if any. Such a criterion is neither logical nor empirical: it is simply based on a given and unquestioned view of the way questions and answers should relate. Unfortunately, the very claim concerning this relationship cannot be reflexively applied to logical empiricism and does not embody this relationship. What counts as a valid answer is not questioned by empiricism, and logical empiricism itself is neither a logical nor an experimental answer to the question of answerhood at large. It explains why logical empiricism is not the general conception of problem solving it claims to be.

Nihilism and positivism have not survived, nor could they. But they have shaped the philosophical horizon of our century by their endeavor to come to grips with the generalized problematicity that we have found everywhere in culture, from painting to music and literature. The old models of thought, the old values, have given way to the conceptualization of their own collapse. They have been radically problematized, and this in itself was supposed to be a sufficient solution, at least for nihilism. In all the cases that we have considered, what is problematic is seen as something negative, to be dissolved if it cannot be solved; and this is true for logical empiricism as well. Problematicity is associated with the crisis, with a rupture and a fragmentation of what has previously constituted a whole.

In this historical context, rhetoric has reemerged. When values are controversial, and experienced as such, it cannot be otherwise. This only proves that rhetoric is the adequate method for treating what is problematic. Rhetoric has an intrinsic relation with questioning, a relation that has never been fully perceived in all its consequences; and we shall have to ask ourselves why that has been the case. The nature of rhetoric itself is involved in such a query.

In reality, all these manifestations mentioned above have exhausted the possibilities contained in their starting points. Rhetoric has supplanted them more and more as the voice of the problematic, though it failed to impose itself in a similar, overall way, probably because questioning and argumentation have continued to bear the same opprobrium which Plato bestowed upon them two millennia ago. The untenability of nihilism and positivism has emerged, as even thinkers like Heidegger and Wittgenstein have granted it, because of an internal contradiction already implied in their act of birth. Nihilism, as much as logicism, rests upon an unquestioned conception of questioning, which, as such, is erroneous. Questioning should be questioned for itself and offer itself as its principle, quite naturally. What is problematic is a positive feature of thought, because it is constitutive of the human mind. One judges a person by the questions he or she raises, as one judges a theory by the questions it solves, or a writing by the question it evokes or compels one to ask.

Problematicity, therefore questioning, should now be questioned for itself, not through some manifestation which distorts it and, in turn, defeats itself due to some initial misrepresentation. Questioning should serve as a new starting point of thought and cease to be viewed as a historical burden. It could spare us from erecting partial conceptions as general ones. With the revival of rhetoric, and for the same reasons, we have observed a renewed interest in questioning (R. G. Collingwood, Hans-Georg Gadamer, Jaakko Hintikka, Esther Goody, et al). But those researches have been pursued in a scattered way. One has failed to see what is grounding, fundamental, and unifying in questioning, which, as a consequence, has not appeared to be more than one field of interest among many others.

Questioning is essentially a difference: the difference between question and answers. I have called it the *problematological difference* because it enables us to provide answers about questioning and still maintain the questioning process. We can have, at the reflexive level, problematological answers that describe and express problems in answer to metaproblems and apocritical answers that give us their solution, also at a second level of speech. The difference is preserved at the level of answers by the indication of the type of answers the locutor offers his audience. If we remember well, the very fact that questions could not be marked off and specifically characterized at the level of the explicit caused the conflation of problematicity and silence. What is problematic cannot be apprehended without the concept of problematological difference, duplicated at the reflexive level. As a result, narratives such as Kafka's *Test* will appear as paradoxical, as absurd, for the simple reason that we cannot make sense of an assertion reducing its content to the expression of the problematic. Such a statement is bound to dissolve itself. Literature, as a matter of fact, has only put into fiction the crisis but also the impossibility of language conceived on the narrow basis of referentiality or deviations with respect to referentiality. We now need a theory of language better adapted to express the problematic in terms other than purely negative ones. A problem should be something other than a mere tract or a vacuous signifier that signifies nothing. It should become possible to answer on what is in question without losing it along the way, thereby falling into paradox, the absurd, the unsayable, or the necessarily fictional. Such a fall is nonetheless bound to happen in the framework of a propositional model of language, against which problematology fights over and over.

A proposition is a neutral concept with respect to questions and answers. The notion of a proposition is the historical product of the negation of questioning. As the basis for a general conception of language, it is bound to be unable to capture the problematic when it finally becomes a cultural and a philosophical imperative. The problematological difference, on the other hand, even enables us to conciliate what can now be retained of logical empiricism and negative metaphysics. Inasmuch as they propose ways of ensuring the problematological difference, they both present valuable indications for us. Obviously, we can answer a question by a proposition which renders the question pointless, as in science. This is one possible way of establishing the problematological difference. Another possible way consists in answering on questions, thereby preserving them and, at the same time, going beyond them. The Hegelian *Aufhebung* is a good example. It is sufficient that questions and answers be demarcated, be recognizable. An answer that repeats a question is nonetheless an answer, and it relates to a real question even if the question remains open through the answer. When an answer bears upon a given problem, the problematological difference is clearly established: the problem *does not have* to vanish from the scene. Both "entities" can be identified, though, quite evidently, not necessarily by syntactical or semantical means. Metaphysical answers are meant to question, therefore to express questions, which, as a result, will not disappear! This shows well enough that neither positivism nor nihilism has been fair to the other, on the basis, precisely, of a very narrow view of questioning (whose roots are to be found in two thousand years of propositionalist tradition). This has affected rhetoric up to its contemporary rebirth.

2. RHETORIC WITHOUT QUESTIONING

The revival of rhetoric is undoubtedly due to the considerable work of Chaim Perelman. Not surprisingly, he attacked logical empiricism and metaphysics, mostly for equivalent reasons from the standpoint of a "new rhetoric." Both defend an absolute overview and an indisputable battery of principles which, in turn, impede discussion at large. They both foster truth as being revealed or unfolded to anonymous readers, who are the passive subjects of inferences, against which no one can appeal. But we should now move beyond exclusion toward integration, because the times themselves have changed. Let us listen to Robert Hanna's review of Perelman's *Realm of Rhetoric:*

> The one major theoretical flaw in the *Realm of Rhetoric* seems to lie in Perelman's treatment of the relation of formal logic and argumentation. These are constantly contrasted, but never unified. On Perelman's view, if argumentation excludes formal logic and if philosophy's proper subject is the theory of argumentation, then it follows that there can be no philosophy of logic. This seems an unhappy consequence. Another lesser difficulty... is Perelman's explicit restriction of argumentation to ethical, political and legal domains. This seems to suggest that there is no argumentation in aesthetics or religion.[10]

Rhetoric should integrate logic as well as literature if it aims at establishing itself as a universal approach to problems. Where does the idea that rhetoric deals with opposite propositions come from, if not from the assumption that there is always a question with alternative answers which underlies and defines the nature of the opposition of two positions? But problems have seldom been characterized as rhetoric, even in its heyday, even with Perelman, who nonetheless recognized the capital importance of questioning in his discussions of the future and extension of rhetorical reason. The definition of rhetoric by the audience and its assent is bound to maintain rhetoric in the waters of relativism. The notion of the universal audience does not help much. It cancels out the subjectivism associated with the idea of audience, but, on the other hand, it ceases to be an operational concept, since it can only be understood as a metaphor. If it is the rhetorical translation of the old concept of Reason, what have we gained with rhetoric that we did not already have? The features of the universal audience will remain necessarily indeterminate; it will serve, at best, as a sort of Kantian regulative idea whose purpose is to give rhetoric an objectivity it would otherwise be deprived of. Rhetoric cannot ground objective validity in an imaginary audience that nobody in particular can impersonate. Problems arise out of given situations and are such for given persons. The laws of questioning, however, possess a validity which does not depend either on the latter or on the former. Moreover, we need a theory of language in which, from logic to literature in passing by everyday situations, problematicity is dealt with. This general theory purports to unify, but also to give an objective ground to rhetorical reason. We should rather acknowledge that rhetoric deals with problems, but this is not solely what rhetoric does. This is why I speak of problematology.

When Perelman wrote *The Realm of Rhetoric* in 1977, he still saw questioning as a mere subsidiary and limited technique, following in this respect a long tradition of disgrace put on questioning by Plato and Aristotle. Most specialists have not yet fully realized that the condemnation of rhetoric by Plato coincides with the devaluation of questioning and its unavoidable assimilation with sophistic. The propositional model gives a privilege to truth. What can be "truer" than mathematical or scientific theories? What can be more fallacious than propositions which are neither true nor false, because they are debatable? The propositional model, in rhetoric, is self-defeating. This is why we need a conception of language based on questioning. Rhetoric did not find it necessary, however, to formulate such a conception. The main reason is that its area does not limit itself to language, but to law or ethics, where values, not discourse, are in question. But this is a wrong argument; besides, it has the damaging consequence of letting go undiscussed the propositional model, which precludes any advancement of rhetoric, whose object is problems rather than assertions whose truth-values are to be decided once and for all as the relevant and essential feature. If rhetoric deals with questions settled by a judge or conflicts of opinion regulated by common sense or a prevailing code of conduct, it is because, each time, a problem is to be solved. Something is in question and, as a consequence, in need of a solution. When people resort to language, they also work out some question they have in mind. To Perelman's example of the expert who wants to convince an audience and therefore does not resort to questioning,[11] I shall reply in the following way.

Adherence seems to be a subjective phenomenon, deprived of any law of functioning. In fact, we can define persuasion problematologically. Persuasion is the fact that the locutor has answered the questions raised by the audience, or those the audience has in mind. This does not imply that the audience becomes an interlocutor and explicitly addresses a question to the locutor. Let me risk another conceptualization: the *force* of an argument. An argument is all the more convincing for a given person (or group of persons) when this person is led to draw the conclusion for himself (or herself). The force of an argument varies directly with the freedom left to the addressed individual: the arguments that are imposed are seldom convincing; an argument is all the stronger when the addressee is free to reject it. Let us take a brief example. A says to B: "Is not John dishonest?" He could more bluntly affirm "John is dishonest." But he does not proceed that way, because he wants to give a greater force to his opinion. When A raises the above rhetorical question, he does not want to be responsible for formulating the accusation he has in mind. He does not wish to be accused, in turn, of slander. *With respect to B,* on the other hand, A will be all the more convincing when he elicits the answer from B instead of giving it to him authoritatively. B has the possibility to reject A's presupposed opinion of John; but he is *asked* to deal with the question, and he will evidently believe it all the more when he will have produced it himself, instead of having merely heard it. By letting our interlocutors draw the inference, instead of deriving the conclusion ourselves, we afford them the opportunity to make *theirs* the conclusion, by a sort of process of appropriation or, from our point of view, of transfer.

At the end of the spectrum, we have the mere evocation of a question embedded in a text, a question that the writer does not directly raise to the reader. Reading, too, is a questioning-process, since it forces the reader to confront himself with what is in question in the text. This is why an expert does not have to resort to explicit questioning in order to convince an audience, though he will not be able to convince it if he does not address himself to the questions the audience has in mind or is interested in. A forceful argumentation will also deal with all the relevant subquestions related to problems which are debated (the second complementary criterion of the force of the argument) and will provide an answer, thereby precluding any (explicit or mental) calling into question, i.e., dissent. In sum, the force of an argument increases according to two factors: thoroughness and transfer of inference; science is therefore convincing, as much as any implication rooted in an everyday situation.

Let us now go back to rhetoric without questioning, which is the view of rhetoric associated with the propositional model of thought and judgment. The dissociation of questioning and rhetoric could only lead to the assimilation of rhetoric with sophistic, thereby justifying Plato's condemnation. Opposition of propositions must be seen as something negative according to the propositional model, since a question at stake cannot be reduced to a true proposition or a set of true propositions. The propositional aspect is quite unessential to the true characterization of rhetoric. On the other hand, the rejection of rhetoric can be validated if questioning is debased. This is why any dissociation of questioning and rhetoric, as practiced by the propositionalists since Plato, has always compelled rhetoric to prove that it was more than a technique to establish truth. The autonomy of rhetoric was then impossible, as well as the proof, for rhetoric to be more than the servant of the propositional claims.

Rhetoric is a discourse in which one can hold opposite judgments on the same question. What is problematic remains so through the displayed multiplicity of judgments. We find the same multiplicity in language, and it is called polysemy. Equivocality and the existence of a plurality of answers, which lie at the core of rhetorical debate, are intrinsically related. An equivocal answer to a question is not the answer to that question, since other answers are equally possible. The question is then left unsolved. An equivocal answer is not an answer, or, rather, it is another expression for the problem: it is a problematological answer, since it is a statement which calls for a further discussion of the question. But we have to conclude. Conclusive assertions should really, and not fallaciously, end the debate by providing *one* answer. The question is then solved and does not repeat itself at the assertoric level. Fixed meanings, definitions, and the like will be an *a priori* condition of univocity in language. Questions that arise will then emerge from what is intrinsically problematic, not from linguistic ambiguities. A true question, in Plato's sense, is therefore rooted in reality, which causes the emergence of the question. Ontology and rhetoric have emerged in reaction against one another. But reality is not problematic. If what is known turned into its opposite, knowledge would then remain the same, since a problematic proposition implies the possibility of its denial. The knowledge of the problematic is not knowledge at all, since what is known could still be different, if not totally something else, but its corresponding knowledge would be left unchanged. Where would be the adequacy of both on such a view of knowledge? If questions arise during the knowing process, it cannot be out of the real itself: they do not have objective necessity, or, to use a less anachronistic vocabulary, questions do not have ontological bearing. As a consequence, questioning can only be rhetorical, never epistemological. This is confirmed, in Plato's eyes, with the famous paradox of the *Meno:* if I know what I look for, it is useless to look for it; and if I do not know what I look for, it is really impossible to find it, since I have no idea what to look for. The progress of knowledge has then nothing to do with questioning. Questions are mere rhetorical devices that trigger knowledge to be recalled to the mind.

This view has had tremendous consequences on questioning, on the conceptualization of knowledge, and on rhetoric for more than two thousand years. Questions are used to trigger preexisting knowledge. This implies that propositions exist anteriorily and that they "express" them nonassertorically: questions are rhetorical triggers with respect to propositions. They serve as a means to elicit judgments, whose validity as judgments, their truth, stems only from other judgments. Propositionality and validity, hence truth, form an equation. Judgments, being related to one another, define what has been known since then as *deductive connections.* Even though propositions emerge as answers, answerhood is an unessential feature of propositions because it refers to the rhetoric of their *discovery* and not to the justification, which alone counts. The propositional model is born, and with it the rejection of questioning as a rhetorical trigger and knowledge as justification of propositions. Truths are established as such, independently of the questions they answer. They are but the interrogative form (rhetoric = form) of judgments whose primacy has now imposed itself. Questioning pertaining to rhetoric, instead of the reverse, precluded a problematology from being constituted, but it also led to the subjection of rhetoric to the propositional model. On such grounds, rhetoric was bound to become assimilated with eristic, since the ideal of justification is the absolute necessity provided by metaphysics and the deductive mode of inference, as in logic and mathematics. Rhetoric, as part of the propositional system of thought, is minimized, but it can also be seen as a kind of intellectual perversion. If we play with propositions, if we debate, not questions, but the *truth of assertions,* the very fact that we cannot establish the *true proposition* to be retained against any other shows that rhetoric goes against the basic requirements of proposition theory. Proposition theory is better served by logic. The main relevant attribute of a proposition is its truth-value. Rhetoric does not seem to be much concerned with truth, since it admits opposing views concerning theses. It therefore allows for false assertions to be admitted. When rhetoric is seen as the confrontation between propositions, it cannot be demarcated from sophistic, since one of the characteristics of a sophist is that he can defend opposite theses.

Sophistic, as much as it is rejected by philosophy, is the enemy of rhetoric. Rhetoric without questioning as a guiding principle is merely a subjective enterprise. By rejecting Plato's rejection of questioning, we shall break the conflation of rhetoric and sophistic. Unfortunately, rhetoricians have always neglected questioning, as if they accepted, by ignorance or easiness, Plato's criticisms. But those criticisms have had the far-reaching consequences that have caused rhetoric, still today, to be considered as a mere technique, ranging from seduction to political manipulation. Rhetoric cannot be isolated, and the problematological turn is meant to restore the philosophical value of rhetoric, along with other goals.

3. THE PROBLEMATOLOGICAL CONCEPTION OF LANGUAGE

People resort to language because they have a problem in mind. In doing so, they are then confronted, whatever that problem, with the problematological difference which institutes the minimal requirement defining the solution. This difference does not tell, in each particular case, when we have a solution, nor what it should be. It simply states that solutions should be demarcated from their corresponding questions, that a solution which would not be marked off from the problem it answers would duplicate it and would not solve it at all. An answer which would duplicate a problem is naturally called a problematological answer, but to be an answer at all, it should relate to *two* different problems: the one expressed and the other it is meant to answer, whose object is the former problem. The problematological difference establishes the conditions of a solution, as well as its recognizability, not its obtaining.

The first and most immediate way by which locutors relate to their problems with language is by declaring their solution, i.e., what they think about that question. The very fact of speaking implies that the locutor raises a question thereby. The hearer, who does not necessarily know which question the locutor had in mind, must discover it. Grammar fulfills this purpose. It often enables us to know to which question what it said relates. For instance, if I say "Napoleon lost at Waterloo" it means the same as "Napoleon is the person *who . . .*" and so forth. When the locutor thinks that the question he has in mind can be understood with his sentence, he will not use interrogatives to specify which question he has thereby addressed (i.e., what he precisely meant). If he thought the opposite, he would use as many interrogative clauses as he deemed necessary. On the other hand, an interlocutor can always *actually* raise the question of the meaning of some element of the sentence or of the whole utterance. The answer will then take up the question as being answered: "Napoleon won at Austerlitz" is then semantically equivalent with "Napoleon is the general *who* won at Austerlitz."

In other words, what is explicit, being an answer, raises the issue of to which question it is the answer. Language users are very much aware of all this. Even if they do not thematically know the problematological theory of language, they constantly apply it. Let us take two examples, the first borrowed from politics, the other from psychoanalysis. Imagine two candidates for the White House. One of them affirms of the other: "No, John Smith is not a crook!" By denying the dishonesty of his opponent, the first candidate obviously raises the question of the honesty of his rival and thereby suggests that it *could* be asked. His answer is meant to cast suspicion. We could multiply similar examples. If some local official claims that there are good police officers in his town, then he calls into question the efficiency of the whole police department. Would he say that, if there were not some less-good officers? At any rate, the question is thereby under the attention of the addressees.

As to psychoanalysis, the best illustration is given by Freud himself in his paper on *Verneinung* (denial or negation). If somebody says "I have nothing against you," it may be true, but the very fact that he says what he says evokes the question to which the affirmation replies. The addressee realizes that the locutor *could* have something against him. The statement of friendliness is then called into question, for verification. Freud's claim is stronger: those statements affirm the opposite of what they seem to mean. They are rhetorical precautions. The mechanism of denial is the following: if the question did not arise by the locutor's answer, he would not even address it. Since the locutor answers the question by rejecting it as irrelevant, he contradicts himself; the denial, then, destroys itself in favor of the opposite answer. The problematological difference is established at the level of the explicit, for the question remains implicit. But such is not always the case. In many circumstances, the problem has to be expressed because the solution has to be brought by the addressee. As a consequence, the problematological difference must be formally, explicitly respected. What is declared is the solution; therefore, nondeclarative forms will be used to express the problems. Imperative and interrogative forms specify the type of cooperation required or simply taken from the addressee. Form is then the means by which the problematological difference characterizes language. But quite often, when interlocutors meet in a given context, they share a lot of information on the topic they discuss (the question is then associated with *topoi*), and they know a lot of what the other knows. These *topoi* are what is out-of-the-question in the question itself. So is embodied the problematological difference. The context contains the question and the "out-of-question," which are the presuppositions of the question. They enable the locutor to *say* (problem or solution) something which will be understood by the addressee. As a result, the *topoi,* shared by the protagonists of the speech-act, enable them to differentiate what is problematic from what is not. The constraint of form will then be loosened. We can even say, on the basis of the principle stated above, that the more the context is topically rich in information, the less form has to institute the problematological difference. The answers are univocal, and questions are decidable, unless explicitly and problematologically demonstrated as unprovable (Kurt Gödel). Context plays a mere expository role, not a constitutive one, for logical discourse and for science at large. Form has then a major role to play, as we all know.

On the contrary, in everyday situations forms are more flexible. A question such as "Will you please pass the salt?" is the interrogative form for a simple request of cooperation. The problem has no verbal solution, because the interrogative form does not express an epistemic question. In this example, the form is codified: there is no context in which this form can suggest a verbal answer. What is important to notice is that the problematological difference is ensured by means other than form when the context allows it. This *law of complementarity* finds one of its confirmations in the possibility for interrogative sentences to express assertions ("Is he not dishonest?"), but also for assertions to have an interrogative force ("I ask myself whether John will come tomorrow"). The law of complementarity explains why, more generally, we can mean something other than what the form literally stipulates in a given context. In such a complementarity between form and context, as a mode of problematological differentiation, we find the splitting of meaning into the literal and the figurative. The literal meaning is formally so. It tells us what a given sentence is *expected* to tell us, independently of the circumstances of its utterance. These circumstances may confirm the literal reading as being the sole one intended by the locutor. But the literal reading can also be used as a mediation for another one. It can function as a trigger for an unexpected, contextualized interpretation. The context can serve as a *problematizer* for the assertion, which now becomes *problematic* for the interlocutor, who has to supply the answer himself instead of merely receiving it with respect to his own questions. The questioner, who is also an addressee, must now supplement in response to this otherness *implied* by the assertion uttered. In a sentence such as "It is one o'clock," it may be *implied* "Let's have lunch." Conversational implications are, as we see, modalities of argumentative inferences, which, in turn, presuppose the dualization of meaning. Only the context will enable one to supply the correct answer to what is meant by "It is one o'clock." The declarative sentence "It is one o'clock" can be used to say something other than the mere phrase to what is literally in question in the propositions-content of that phrase. The relative autonomization of propositions is one of their problematological features: it comes from the role of context as a way of ensuring the problematological difference. Then, forms are not essential to meet this requirement. Forms can live a life of their own, so to speak, and they can have a contextualized reading. Assertions can evoke, suggest, imply other assertions in virtue of their effective problematization in reading or counterargumentation. Assertions, being not solely answers, are therefore problematological too with respect to questions other than those they solve.

4. LITERARY RHETORIC

Deliteralization of the form, in language, is conditioned by the transfer of problematological differentiation upon the context. In literature, however, the duality of meaning is a structural feature.[12] But there is a context in which locutor and interlocutor share *topoi,* besides those to be found in the wide repertoire defined by an identical community, understood in a broad sense. The basic difference between literature and everyday language—another task for problematology, which must deal with questions of logic as much as with the "logic" of literature—is the relation with the context. Auto-contextualization is the means by which literature enables itself to play with forms. Fiction incorporates a description of the context that would be implicit in everyday situations. That is why it is fiction. The reader has to know some contextual elements of the situation. We even find that kind of description in the *nouveau roman.* Let us quote the opening of *Les Gommes,* by Alain Robbe-Grillet: "Dans la pénombre de la salle de café le patron dispose les tables et les chaises, les cendriers, les siphons d'eau gazeuse." All this need not be said when we see the situation. Similar examples could be multiplied. Novelists have always to describe what, in usual contexts, is never made explicit, in order to make the context known to the reader. In other words, they create their own context in the text, as a text. The question is to know how the problematological difference will be respected. What will become of the law of complementarity in fiction, since there are only formal means to ensure the difference between problems and solutions? Fiction, too, deals with problems, with questions. In this respect, literature has not changed very much since the Greeks. Ann Jefferson, in her excellent book *The Nouveau Roman and the Poetics of Fiction,* is quite clear on this feature I have called the auto-contextualization of the problematic: "These two genres, the detective story and Greek tragedy, both depend heavily on a delayed truth which is only revealed at the end. Both genres are highly theological and seem to conform closely to the structural norm which emerged from the foregoing discussion of narrative organization."[13] In fact, narrative organization defines itself as the staging of a problematic, which ends in a revelation of its solution. Let us listen to Jefferson again:

> Robbe-Grillet picks up this theme of the final truth and alludes to it in the epigraph of *Les Gommes:* "time, which sees to everything, has given the solution, despite you," a version of two lines from Sophocles' tragedy.... In both the original and the altered form, these lines emphasize the notion of (inevitable) revelation, be it in the form of *solution* (to an enigma) or *disclosure* (of a truth). The novel itself, however, fails to reveal anything or to solve any mystery. The detective, instead of uncovering the murderer, commits the crime himself at the end of his inquiry. As Jean Ricardou says, "the inquiry *precedes* the murder and, in preceding it, *engenders* it." This is the reverse of *Oedipus the King.* ... In *Les Gommes,* mysteries are multiplied rather than solved. The novel constantly invites us to ask "why," but then declines to answer. If the detective aspect of the novel proves unfruitful, one might look for narrative coherence in another strand.[14]

What does this passage suggest about the rhetorical nature of fiction? Problematicity used to refer to a given solution within the text. Detective stories and "gothic novels" still embody problem and solution in the plot. The characteristic of modern literature is that, more and more, the problem does not receive a solution. The problem is described, narrated, textualized for its own sake, as an object in itself. The literary answer has then become a problematological answer: the problem is the subject of fiction, just like consciousness. Philosophy being unable to provide a problematology, no wonder that literature, which can rhetoricize problems, presents so much interest for philosophers nowadays. Literature is more and more enigmatic. This is why, in a sense, Kafka's piece illustrates so well the rhetoricization of literature by itself and therefore its character as an escape from everyday reality. But auto-referentiality is a consequence of a generalized problematicity as we have described it. It cannot be isolated as a property of language at large, but as a possibility among others, and it cannot be taken for a basis of a general theory of literature, as deconstruction has claimed. Problematology does not deny auto-referentiality but explains it with principles which go far beyond the sphere of literature.[15] The concept of problematological difference enables us to understand why solutions, in the traditional sense of the term, being more absent from literature, are equated with the problems themselves, and why such a shift leads to an increased "formalization" in poetry as well as in prose. When previous solutions become problems in the intellectual horizon of a given period, the problematic remains the only possible solution left. The problematological difference must be respected. In detective stories, the solution can be demarcated from the problem quite clearly. The problem is specified from the beginning, and as a beginning; the solution comes afterward. *Time is inscribed in textuality as a progression from problem to solution, as a discovery.* This is why time-breaks create a feeling of problematicity: the progression from the problem to its solution is broken. And the more enigmatic a text is, the more the reader is solicited to deal with the question. The reader has to bring about the consistency of textual synthesis because the text itself does not answer something other than the problem it fictionalizes in some other way. The problematicity of the text calls for an answer that the reader has to give. This is how I explain the major importance taken by the phenomenology of reading in the contemporary analysis of literature. Wolfgang Iser's *Act of Reading* is a masterpiece in this respect.

When the context is embodied in the text, the latter bears the whole weight of ensuring problematological differentiation. As a result, if the problem is explicitly specified, the problematological difference emerges out of the literal reading progressively, i.e., comes out of the literalization of the text. Figurative form is minimal. The problematological difference is textually marked, quite literally. The text does not say, of course, that it *does* enact that difference because it is the nonliteral result of reading. Since textuality, in this case, literalizes the progress from problem to solution and their demarcation at the level of the explicit, figurative language is minimal. Form plays the role of stipulating, usually in everyday terms, situations which are normally tacitly experienced. Hence the increased need for adequacy between word and world. The language which is used will be highly mimetic, as expected from our usual language practice, which must refer and transfer.

As to the reader, he is taken by or into the story once the problem becomes his (hence the "willing suspension of disbelief"). The narrative is meant to unfold the solution. The highly mimetic function of such narratives is ensured through form. Literality and referentiality are closely associated: the former creates the illusion of reality through the latter. One could ask in which way language associates referentiality and answerhood, taken from a literal point of view. I shall deal in Chapters 4 and 5 with my theory of judgment, and with the deletion of interrogatives which grounds the synthesis of subject and predicate. What is important to note for the time being is that the interrogative theory of judgment as answer has a counterpart, a theory of the sentence and its meaning; both subvert the traditional way of looking at the judgment which has prevailed since Plato and Aristotle and still feed the logicians' debates. In my book *Meaning and Reading* I have shown how literality, as a feature of sentences, creates referentiality, that is, a sense of relatedness to the correlates of interrogatives, deleted or not, underlying the elements of sentences. Names, for instance, refer as the referential items designated by interrogatives, present or not (through relative clauses), such as *who, what, where,* and *when.* Deliteralization, on the other hand, has an inverse effect. It engenders a *retreat from mimesis,* as I call it. In other words, the reader is compelled to dualize reading and go beyond a literal interpretation deemed as impossible. Referentiality ceases to be the solution to the question of meaning. The mimetic, or referential, reading of the text must then be abandoned. Problematicity is not resolved by the literal elements of answerhood, as given by the answers of the text itself. Those answers are problematic, in spite of the fact that they are answers. Hence, the less a problem is literally marked, in the literary solution, the more it has to be formally differentiated.

Form—and such a concept means textuality and its organization—will bear the weight of ensuring the problematological difference. How else could the problematic be marked in the literary solution? By *form,* I mean all the language devices used by the writer, such as style, sentence ordering, play with syntax, and the like. Let us recall that we have no context ready at hand and that it has to be created within the text itself. Form has, then, a maximal role to play in this matter, according to the law of complementarity. As a result, symbols will be more widely used as textual riddles which express the fictional quest. Figurative language will be more widely used to serve the rhetorical purpose of problematizing the reader. The textual solution will be increasingly open to multiple readings in virtue of the problematicity it embodies. Problematicity implies multiplicity, i.e., equivocality. In order to grasp the derived, or implied, meaning, the reader cannot limit his own questioning to the mere progressive reading, which is often broken by various rhetorical devices used by the author. Figurative reading can only result from the reader's own work, from his own quest, achieved by an effort of interpretation that the text itself does not offer at a first reading. The latter must be dereferentialized, and verisimilitude ceases to be the key of fiction; hence the retreat from mimesis which is a general feature of modern fiction in its most creative trends. Poetry, for instance, becomes more esoteric and is less and less realistic, even when it deals with human emotions, which are, thus, allegorized more than described.

Literary solution has now become the expression of the problematic itself. The enigmatic is the form itself. This explains why literature is auto-referential. It has very little to do with Saussure's theory of the arbitrariness of the sign, which is the theoretical pretext of deconstructivism. The problem is the absence present in the literary enigma, a mere form, a solution calling for something else. The very possibility of such a process is a manifestation of the problematological difference. It is, in fact, the problematological difference itself as experienced at the crossroads of historicity and auto-contextualization. The latter is literature; the former, the increased sense of time as it goes by and puts into question what was considered as going without saying at an earlier epoch. The problematization of that which was considered as literally out-of-the-question has become questionable at the very level of principles. Adequacy with the real requires its problematization, hence, in fiction, an auto-contextualized and increased formulation of the problematic. Literary solutions, then, undergo a retreat from mimesis, which nonetheless expresses the most realistic requirements, because reality is problematic as a culture system in contemporary culture. Everydayness can be described, and is bound to be (maybe as never before), but as something opaque and rather enigmatic in its subjectively "grounded" interrelatedness.

If literary theory belongs to rhetoric as I conceive of it, it is because literature represents problems and solutions in various ways, in a proportion conditioned by problematicity as experienced in the "real world," as borrowed from, or imposed by, this world. Vladimir Propp's functions used to describe folktales are nothing but "problematic expressions." Tragedy, too, contains such problematic situations, and it is only in the contemporary modes of fiction that, maybe, such a problematicity is less apparent because only formal. This is probably because we think of problematicity as a content. "In the mode of narration," writes Zahava McKeon,

we derive thought and action from characters and predicaments
of which agents are not fully aware, but which they come to
recognize as problematic situations to be resolved. However,
since the discoveries which resolve problematic situations are
also insights into themselves as agents, resolution of a problematic situation leads to new predicaments and new complications.
Consequently, an affirmative reading implies the legitimacy of a
tragic reading as well.[16]

A "solution" ensures the progress of fiction, but nothing in the nature of
fiction implies that such solutions should prevail. Modern fiction, rather,
thematizes the problematic, leaving thereby open-ended the story if any.
This is rendered possible in virtue of the problematological difference
being marked out otherwise, reflexively (auto-referentially) so to speak.
There is no progress anymore in such a type of fiction.

The rhetorical nature of fiction stems from the fact that alternatives
are open, sometimes deliberately left open. Something is *in question* in
what is said, and it is debated through the solutions proposed, represented, and staged. And what is an argument if not a discourse on a given
question, whether via subquestions (i.e., a story) or not?

The image that we have of arguments goes against such a view. It has
created the scission between poetics and rhetoric. No wonder that literary rhetoric, especially in France, has claimed to be more authentic than
argumentation, which deals with weak inferences (and logic with strong
ones); literary rhetoric cannot be compared negatively with anything
else. "This is a conception of rhetoric divorced from persuasion, from
reference outward to audience."[17] Hence, "a curious paradox remains
unresolved. In rhetoric, criteria must be found in reference to audience;
how then is structural rhetorical criticism possible, since structure is
intrinsic to a literary work while rhetoric would seem to be extrinsic,
viewing the work in light of criteria located outside the work, in audience?"[18] In fact, audience is not an adequate criterion for rhetoric; as I
said before; but now I want to add that to keep that criterion opens the
road to unwanted consequences.

Audience is a concept that sanctions the divorce of argumentation
from all other forms of question-solving processes and autonomizes it
with respect to everything else. Argumentation, as a mere endeavor to
persuade an audience, is a form, a technique. Hence, it is a minor, if not
dangerous, process of thought. This is the historical attitude toward
rhetoric which has prevailed since Plato.

Do rhetoricians really want the traditional *reaction* of rejection to be maintained, *which can only ensue from such a narrow view of rhetoric?* Shall we go on working with the limitations put on rhetoric as argumentative (i.e., persuasive) reasoning, when we *know* that they can only lead to a reduction of what we want rhetoric to be? Argumentation as an audience-oriented reasoning process leaves too much out and amounts to little more than manipulative discourse. Plato defined, or confined, rhetoric to that, but *we* do not have to go along. Argumentation is a concept that, on those terms, represses the problematological nature of rhetoric.

5. ARGUMENTATION AS A PROBLEMATOLOGICAL INFERENCE

All this discussion of literary theory may seem to have led us astray from what is usually called argumentation, namely, reasoning and inference. This is the definition of argumentation which we have inherited from Aristotle; hence, the usual confrontation with logic. To neglect literature and to consider only logical reasoning is the worst thing that could happen to rhetoric: it amounts to a death sentence. Rhetoric being the voice of the problematic, the negation of the problematic on account of the propositional model has the effect of making rhetoric a pure form without substance. If, on account of this model, the justification of unequivocal truth is the aim of rhetoric, rhetoric cannot be but eristic, since it does not deal with truth nor with unequivocal propositions. This has been Plato's main line of thought. Dialectic was supposed to be scientific, and, at the same, it had to retain some question-answer process. Aristotle broke the link: dialectic could be rhetorical and acquire a status of its own, if science was something else. The restoration of dialectic simply completes the movement of idealization of science, demonstration, as being *the* model of rationality. Rhetoric and dialectic could not be assimilated with scientific justification anymore: they could then be studied for themselves.

I do think that those who have told us that Aristotle restored the importance of rhetoric against Plato, by studying it, have really failed to see that Plato and Aristotle shared the same feeling about rhetoric. Plato could not theoretize it, but the same can be said about him when we consider what he did not do with the scientific syllogism. In both cases, Aristotle provided the theory. Plato could not achieve it because for him dialectic *was* scientific: ideas and their division were at the same time "objective" (hence, "scientific"), and "subjective," by the appeal he made to reminiscence and the dialogical game of question and answer. But for Aristotle, too, rhetoric is a propositional process, even when, as in the last book of the *Topics,* it is a question-and-answer relationship. Is not a question a proposition put interrogatively, as he says in *Topics* I, 4, 101b30–38?

In reality, we cannot understand the nature of inference with the propositional model, however strange this seems to be. Inference is a discursive arrangement, and, as such, the problematological difference is at work here too. The truth is that logic without rhetoric is inconceivable. J. S. Mill, like Descartes, attacked logic on account of its sterility— that is, because it is impossible for logic to conclude anything new that is not already contained in the premises. In other words, logic is *question-begging;* nothing is solved with logic, unless, of course, we admit that logic solves problems posed outside logic, as Aristotle already suggested in the *Topics.* In this case, we do not have in logic the problem and the solution, but only the solution. The problem lies in a rhetorical necessity to *resort* to logic. The propositional conception of inference, which fails to see anything but propositions and connections of propositions, will necessarily profess a sterile view of logic and of inference. Once inference is seen as an embodiment of the problematological difference, rhetoric will cease to be debased and logic overvalued against all reasonable criticisms.

To show this, let us suppose that two propositions constitute an inference: then they bear a relationship with each other. Otherwise, the conclusion could not be stated as a conclusion. We then expect to find two conditions satisfied: the two propositions must be different; the conclusion must derive from the first in such a way that we cannot arrive at an opposite proposition. To conclude B from A means that A enables us to establish B rather than not-B.

All this is well known, and even fairly obvious. Let us now suppose that the first condition is not respected. The deduction is vitiated by the conflation of the premise and the conclusion. What is last is first, and conversely. We have then a circle, a vicious one, because the inference is invalidated by the nondifferentiation. We have not progressed from the known to the unknown, from the problematic to the answer, but we have abolished that difference. In other words, we have *begged the question.* The constitutive factor of an inference is, therefore, that it establishes a problematological differentiation.

The premise is out-of-the-question and the conclusion is problematic; or the reverse, if we prefer *analysis* to *synthesis.* The relevant fact is the requirement of the problematological difference. Inference settles a question by means of another proposition. It is an implication, as much as "It is one o'clock" implies "Let's have lunch!" Syllogistic inference excludes alternatives (A, then B, and not-B is excluded), whereas rhetorical inference, or argumentation, leaves several possibilities open most of the time.

We have now a general conceptualization for inference at large: to infer is to solve a question via another one that it expresses. When we say "It is one o'clock," and we want our interlocutor to conclude "Let's have lunch!" the process of inference is the following: our answer on time raises another question whose answer is the conclusion. On a contextual basis, the addressee infers the second answer from the first, because the context enables him to treat the first answer as problematological of another question than the one it literally replies to.

Duality of meaning, based on the context, or on the sole text, creates an implication: A is a sign of B, whether not-B, C, D, etc., are excluded is not at stake here. In literature, as much as in logic, we *infer.* There is no difference *in principle* between logical inference, rhetorical inference, and literary interpretation. In all these cases, a problem is in question, and its problematological expression calls for another answer; whether or not it be the sole possible one does not matter here, even though it does make the difference between logic, rhetoric, and literature.

Causal relationship and weak propositional ties are therefore variations along the line of possible question-answer relationship, i.e., inferences. Interpretation is inference as much as logical reasoning, and argumentative reasoning cannot be cut off from either, as they are in the propositional model of thought, according to which propositions are the sole units, through reduction, and therefore truth should be the sole measure of inference. This model necessarily implies heterogeneity for literary rhetoric and weakness for argumentation when compared to logic which establishes truth univocally. A sign implies as much to the extent that it indicates something else which is discovered as an inferential relation: A being given, B ensues. Inference has always this structure, whatever the refinements.

What is a syllogism? It is a propositional difference which cannot be explained on the basis of the propositional model. Why should we resort to two propositions in order to establish another one? Why is inference impossible when we conflate the premises and the conclusion, i.e., when we beg the question? Why is "reasoning a discussion in which, certain things having been laid down, something other than these things necessarily results through them?" (*Topics,* I, 100a25). The answer to all the above questions cannot be provided by a theory of propositions but only by a theory of questioning, since only there do we find a ground for not conflating question and answer, i.e., for instituting a difference in order to arrive at an answer. Now if we stick to the propositional conception of thinking, not only do we have to accept the primacy of a given *model* (i.e., ideal) as evident, but we also have to face the debasement of any reasoning which does not conform, such as is the case with argumentation. Since the latter is qualitatively different, we do not account for it positively, but as a departure from the initially accepted rule.

Problematology does not deal with logic, i.e., "strong" inference, which can neither explain itself nor validate its so-called evidence, but it can affirm that all forms of inference are embodiments of the problematological inference. But this is already the problem addressed in Chapter 3.

3

Toward a Rhetoric of Reason

1. OLD AND NEW RHETORIC

I t is customary to oppose logic to argumentation, just as it goes without saying that the latter differentiates itself from literary rhetoric. This tradition, born with Aristotle, was faithfully followed by Perelman, who brought rhetoric back to its proper place by going beyond the logical empiricism then prevailing.

Argumentation has never ceased to be anything but a weak inference, noncompelling in its conclusions, which must be brought to life in countering the monopoly of demonstrative or apodictic inference represented by logic. As a result of this negative definition of the rhetorical field, rhetoric finds itself *ab initio* in a position of inferiority, not to say on the defensive. And thus it is necessary to discern just what the reduction of rhetoric to a conflict between propositions signifies. Yet the goal remains, as in logic, a conclusion about truth and the justification of its acceptance. But in this game, logic is without a doubt more efficient, since its conclusions are without appeal: its propositions are true, and known as such, as are the indisputable justifications of their truth-values. Argumentation, which also deals with propositions, i.e., truth-values, can thus be no more than a substitute, appropriate in nonscientific contexts before any scientific decision can take place. The least one can say is that rhetoric finds itself in a position of inferiority since it is situated well short of the establishment of truth; in any case, rhetoric cannot settle once and for all alternative theses in opposition.

We should equally note the underlying idea behind the propositional model: it combines truth and justification. Not only is science privileged, but the idea itself of truth implies that its possession justifies its acceptance beyond any possible debate. The exclusion of the rhetorical field goes along with this idea of truth. Truth is convincing "as such," hence the superiority of any procedure which establishes truth univocally over any thought process, which debates without establishing one conclusion in a decisive and necessary way, and which makes acceptance subjective instead of placing it in an objective field which constrains and subordinates subjective movements.

Whoever asserts a proposition gives it a truth-value, and whoever speaks of truth conditions intellectual procedure to exclude all which does not lead to it. Rhetoric, on the contrary, works with the conflicts between propositions. If one conceives of rhetoric as a possible procedure for deciding between propositions, it will inevitably be inferior to science and to logic, which are conclusive. In turn, rhetoric will also be external to the literary field, since literature does not argue. As to science, it is situated beyond all argumentation by virtue of its method of justifying propositions. Scientific method can resolve any opposition by *reductio ad absurdum*. Since any proposition must in principle be true or false, science must be the ideal of the propositional model even when one is still at the (inferior) level where one does not really have knowledge. In this model of reason, what can the positive role and place of rhetoric be?

Such a conception of rhetoric can be found in Plato, who was able to discredit it easily. It rests on the propositional model of the *logos:* a proposition is a proposition of truth. The debate delays, prevents, or even plays on the nontruth, on the possible plurality of acceptable propositions. If one takes the proposition as the unit of reason, argumentation will of necessity be manipulatory or, in the best of cases, prerational, like a weakness of reason. Argumentation will obviously never succeed in justifying truth in the same way as a science and its logic can, because it operates at a level on which the truth cannot be scientifically decided. If such is not the goal of argumentation, then it is necessarily perverse, since it plays with the propositions in a spirit other than that of establishing truth and excluding error. Argumentation is then, so to speak, a *logos* used against itself.

It is all-important to know whether argumentation aims only at deciding between opposing propositions, by explaining truth; or, to go one step further, to ascertain whether reason limits itself by advancing propositions of truth in order to accumulate others, which will be justified as true. The former constitutes a narrow view of reason. Reason is clearly defined by something other than propositions as bearers of truth-values. But, if the propositional norm is our model, all that is anterior to the establishment of truth, or all that falls outside it, will have a diminished status in the best of cases and a negative one in the worst. The rehabilitation of rhetoric will not be accomplished by simply asserting that it is necessary, any more than by insisting on the need to increase its value and use within that model. It is important to completely subvert this model based on propositions, not simply to circumvent it, leaving it intact as if it were not entirely worn out. Perelman, for example, reinvested rhetoric with an undeniable, but limited, credit, because he limited himself only to separating it from logicism, following Aristotle in this respect. However, the basis of logicism itself was not undermined by Perelman; its monopoly alone was breached, as this involved only the ability of rhetoric to exist alongside logic.

All the difficulty outlined stems from equating propositionalism with Western rationality as we have known it since Plato and Aristotle. Plato presents us with a propositionalist view of the *logos* through his dialectic, which encompasses science. His view is based on the rejection of questioning. Socrates rooted philosophy in interrogation. However, he did not think that one could truly respond. The meaning of the *logos* for him is that our *logos* must be problematic: to seek to escape problematicity is illusory, because every position adopted is bound to be questioned. The rulers of the city govern through their pretense of knowing better than others what is suitable. Socrates, in calling into question their responses, displays their contradictions. A logical impasse *(aporia)* results, which leaves the problem as it is. Above all, the rulers, though they thought themselves to be superior and to know better, see themselves unmasked as equals in problematic knowledge with those whom they govern. This is something for which they would not forgive Socrates. In launching the idea that he knew that he knew nothing, Socrates signed his own death warrant.

For Plato, interrogation had to have another function than to perpetuate itself indefinitely in the impossibility of answer. If one questions, it is for the purpose of getting answers. What does the case of Socrates demonstrate, if not that questioning is merely a rhetorical procedure, that knowledge does not result from it, that knowledge cannot be seen as made of answers, and that it cannot be defined by recourse to interrogation? Is this not what the famous paradox of the *Meno* "proves?" If I know what I seek, to question in order to seek it is useless; if I do not know what I look for, to question becomes impossible. Thus, the role of questioning is to bring forth knowledge otherwise embedded in ourselves, through memory that questions activate. Dialectic is rhetorically interrogative in the sense of expressing rhetorical questions. It is a rhetoric which is useful and possible only in the service of knowledge. That which is antecedent to any question is the knowledge of its object, and this is nothing other than the sought answer, both of which define themselves by reference to the existence of something which underlies the question and which is the object of the answer. This identical reality is what makes the very question possible in order to have any meaning. It is its foundation as much as the criterion of its identification as a question: what is questioned is then identified as some what-ness, independently of the question raised about it. What-ness has become assertorical and ceased to be essentially interrogative. The something that underlies the question and that is the object of the answer has been called *Idea* or *Essence.* Knowledge will thus be propositional, the concept of judgment being neutral as compared to those of question and answer. A question is only the occasion for the appearance of the proposition. Interrogation here is merely a rhetorical form for the proposition. The proposition is an answer, but it is only an ancillary feature of what it really is, and it is so only because it happens to result from an interrogation. A judgment has a validity that is independent of the situation which brings it forth, whereas interrogation is circumstantial; it ensues from a contingent occasion linked to given individuals in a particular situation, and truth cannot depend on it.

For Aristotle, the problem that Plato's dialectic poses necessitates a separation between argumentation and logic. Dialectic ceases to be scientific in order to confine itself within the domain of the rhetorical/argumentative. One cannot put knowledge, which is objective, on the same level as interrogation, which is subjective. The latter is individualistic, in that the questions that one poses are based each time on ignorance, hence on the individual's knowledge. Ignorance varies for each of us, as does each one's knowledge. The validity of this knowledge does not rest on the dialectical game of the questions. If this were not the case, one would have knowledge whose basis would vary according to individuals. The condemnation of relativism excludes the fact that knowledge can stem from questioning. However, what Plato does with dialectic is to connect that which cannot be connected: he connects interrogation, which has a rhetorical role, with Ideas, hence with judgment. Plato has given a way out, an issue to Socratic questioning at the price of rendering impossible an unquestionable and indubitable knowledge, as Descartes pointed out later. That is why Aristotle severs dialectic, and its relationship to interrogation (the thrust of book VIII of the *Topics*), from demonstration, thus compelling him to establish different theories for each one. If rhetoric regains the freedom to be accepted, thanks to that theorizing, it cannot really be said that it gains much esteem. The propositional model is well established, and argumentation as compared to science provides weak demonstrations. One can discern in argumentation the historical ancestor of the concept of discovery, from which the idea of *inventio* stems, that one opposes to conceived justification as really restrictive in what it can produce. Aristotle summed it up well: a problem is only a proposition formulated in another fashion. "The difference between a problem and a proposition is a difference in the turn of phrase" (*Topics*, I, 4). One may even add that Aristotle codifies propositionalism with his conception of subject and predicate. The syllogism will generate a proposition from two others by "apodictic" means. However, there is also a dialectical syllogism; this illustrates very well the universal character of propositionalism, in spite of the diverse ways in which propositions are generated.

2. FROM PROPOSITIONAL RHETORIC TO PROBLEMATOLOGICAL RHETORIC

We have seen how the separation between logic and argumentation was born with Aristotle. The rhetorical function that we highlighted at the heart of propositionalism preceded Aristotle and survived him. We too often forget that Perelman rebels against logicism without radically changing its presuppositions. He simply wants a space for rhetoric. Moreover, he does not change the definition. It remains based on mere contradiction at the core of the propositional field. In taking this approach, he does not see that the opposition does not exist of itself, because no more does one toss a proposition as such in the air, with no problem in view, than one opposes a position without reference to a question to be debated. If there is opposition, it is because the minimum of possible responses to a given question is given by the alternative, which is the contradiction when its terms are considered simultaneously. Similarly, if one speaks or writes, it is because one has a question in mind—not an interrogative sentence, but a problem, as when one speaks of a "question of life or death," or says "That is not the question" with regard to a purely affirmative statement, where no "question" in the grammatical sense of the term was posed.

Clearly rhetoric is subordinated to the study of questioning, to the extent that contradiction between propositions exists only in reference to problems and that the use of discourse in general is made with reference to questions that one has in mind.

This idea is confirmed, moreover, on quite a number of levels. Linguistic argumentation, as described by Jean-Claude Anscombre and Oswald Ducrot, refers to the idea of questioning, though these authors do not recognize it. If one says "The weather is nice but not warm enough," p but q, it is with reference to a question r. For example, in "Are we going to take a walk?" p goes in the direction of r ("We are going to take a walk"), while q goes in the opposite direction. It is of little importance that the connector "but" decides on non-r; it permits settling a question, and that suffices to validate my point.

One can cite more examples without having Ducrot's conception add much, since it is often limited to the use of explicit argumentation markers. If I say "It is one o'clock" to signal that it is time to sit down for lunch, I proceed still to argumentation, because I answer one question via another. In this manner I continue to deal with a question and to propose a response, too, because that is how language usage functions.

Proceeding further, if I say "There are good policemen" I suggest that there are also bad ones, because I pose the question and simultaneously evoke the alternative. If I say to someone "The weather is nice," it is because of the possibility that it might not be so. If a husband on a business trip telephones his wife and tells her, in the course of the conversation, that he is indeed faithful, he simultaneously reveals that a question of fidelity does arise, or did arise for him, which may only serve to unsettle the faithful spouse remaining stoically at home.

In summary, the information that an utterance conveys is a response to a question; the question emerges for the interlocutor through the answer to it. The argumentative effects of language can certainly be reinforced by the explicit markers of an implicit problem, but it is not necessary that it is so, because language by nature and function refers to questions. A single proposition, therefore, has an "argumentative value" as such. Someone saying something immediately raises the question of knowing what he responds to, since to speak is to respond, even if his speaking does not enunciate the question to which he is replying. He implies it with a variable degree of forcefulness and presence. Just as a sentence such as "It is one o'clock" poses the question of what it is that it responds to in the context where a knowledge of the exact time does not pose a problem, so in a comparable manner one encounters the interrogative referral mechanism in the example that my five-year-old son presented me with when I gave him a life belt that, to my utter consternation, he wanted to drag everywhere.

DADDY: To go out to eat pizza, you don't need a life belt.
PATRICK: But I don't want pizza!

The argument is interesting from more than one point of view. To Patrick there is only one question to settle: the fact of not wanting a pizza suffices to justify his keeping the life belt, though neither statement has anything to do with the other, as I indicated to him. If he accepts that the pizza is an argument against the life belt, which is obviously not the case, non-pizza becomes an argument in favor of the life belt. And this is really the problem that Patrick has at the moment.

Besides, and this is another application of the problematological view, one cannot comprehend any better the process that Freud described as "denegation" or "denial" without reference to problematological rhetoric. How can one explain linguistically the idea that "I wish you no harm" or "I have nothing against you" means the opposite, without calling upon a problematological rhetoric? The sentence really says: I suggest the question, "Do I wish to harm you or not?" and I affirm one of the two possible responses, that I wish you no harm; this immediately contradicts itself, since one can hardly see the necessity of bringing up the question if it does not arise. Why belie the reply to a question when it is not relevant? Consequently, the reply vitiates its very content, because it refers back to a question for which it is the reply, though denying it. Hence, the unacceptableness of the reply which defeats itself, with the result that the question that it poses can in fact have only the other alternative as an answer.

In virtue of all this we can thus conclude that to argue is nothing more than to express a position on a question. Logic and argumentation are no longer two distinct realities, one of which would be inferior to the other. They are two modalities of the same process called "questioning." In logic the question is settled in univocal fashion, and one can even find as an answer that a question does not have such a solution (Gödel). When the question does not allow itself such a formalistic resolution, it resolves itself otherwise, but not less relevantly. In reality, responding to a question by sustaining it through contradictory debate, by addressing it as well as its presuppositions (e.g., by rejecting them), is to respond nonetheless, because it respects the criterion which I have called the problematological difference. It suffices that one can distinguish the questions from the responses by articulating the latter on the former in a clear manner. One defines the resolution, i.e., the apocritical field of solution, and one clearly brings it forth in its identity, even if it bears on a question which thus continues to exist through the debate while we reflect upon it. Philosophy differs from daily discourse because of this simple fact. In the case of daily discourse, questions are resolved and are made to disappear. This solution does not amount to reflecting on them. In the case of philosophy, on the contrary, questions are kept alive through discourse, because to philosophize is nothing other than to surrender oneself to a radical problematization and to reflect that same problematization through the answers it suggests.

It is clear in light of the foregoing considerations that rhetoric is not a weakness of reason, whose strength would be logical inference. Reason does not have the proposition, the judgment, as a unit, but rather the problem and the solution. Judgment is a reply, and it is the articulation of this difference that constitutes our rationality.

As long as this has not been recognized, one can err as much about the nature of language as about rhetoric, which is reduced to a merely prevalidating, preverifying propositional opposition. Even this opposition has no meaning outside the question for which it is opposition. Logic also, moreover, involves resolving questions.

3. THE RHETORICAL PRINCIPLE OF FICTION: THE LAW OF COMPLEMENTARITY

There remains the matter of the relationships between literary rhetoric and problematological rhetoric. For Aristotle, dialectic encompassed argumentation as well as poetics, to the precise extent that truth, distinctive to science, is not in question. The distinction, with regard to poetics, stems from the fact that it imitates the true, without penetrating it, whereas the oratorical encounter occurs in a different kind of fiction, which simply situates it outside the true. This double rhetoric does not preclude the two areas moving their separate ways, in mutual ignorance and without each preventing the other from viewing itself as the true rhetoric: Roland Barthes or Chaim Perelman?

However, we can spot in recent literary rhetoric an interest in language that a long tradition of studies of individual authors did not favor. The rhetorical presuppositions that such studies reveal, without being explicit, have become the subjects of study in their turn. Here, once again, the theory of language which emerges is inadequate. It concerns a view, in large measure Saussurian, in which the linguistic signs detach themselves from the extralinguistic reference in order to refer to one another, to connote one another indefinitely. In doing so, the signs deliteralize themselves and the literal meaning becomes the mere accessory of a more subtle symbolism, fictional because it is nonreferential in the manner that daily language in fact is. If the signs possess arbitrary reference and express themselves through the *a posteriori* of the world, then fictional language is necessarily first, whereas referential usage is the thrust imposed upon it to relate it to the world. In the beginning was the trope. Figurative language is no longer derived and literalization follows. Language naturally, so to speak, signifies nothing in particular, but everything in general.

Opposed to this conception is the one that sees in language the possibility of intercourse with the world. The figurative is secondary, a derivation imposed on the literal. Referential use is the key to access to the linguistic realm, hence the importance given to the isolated sentence, which must structurally embody its meaning as truth-conditions.

It does not require a great scholar to recognize that these two theories, as opposite (and supposedly universal) as they claim to be, do not stand up to analysis. One favors text, the other, the sentence, each disregarding the object of explanation of the other while maintaining that it integrates it under the circumstances via a theory of derivation. There is no original type of meaning, either literal or figurative. The duality is itself the result of a specific clarification of the problematological difference. A discourse that one can accept literally is a discourse that relies entirely *a priori* on the antecedent meanings of its parts, preparing us for its global meaning. No problem is created which cannot be resolved by transposing the problem into a response via interrogatives whose syntactic function is to safeguard the meaning. Thus, the sentence "Napoleon is he who won at Austerlitz" says the same thing as "Napoleon is the victor of Austerlitz." One has as many interrogative clauses as questions on the literal meaning of words in the sentence.

Figurative language, on the other hand, appears when discourse is susceptible of saying something else, that is, of referring to the implicit, of upsetting the expectation (i.e., by suggesting a query) that the grammatical constituents lead one to believe. This is achieved by displacing that expectation onto another response. There is no primacy of the literal or, inversely, of the figurative, because all discourse can mean something other than what it says. This is due to the rhetorical nature of language, which consists of raising questions in the answers which are proposed. Duality is intrinsic to linguistic usage, and the "most literal" answer can thus split itself, that is, constitute a question without the reply being a simple duplication through the mere play of replacing constituents. The duality of meaning results from the fact that the reply is problematological, that is, the expression of what is enigmatic. Instead of being the reply to an external question, the reply enunciates a problem whose response must be sought outside itself: the question of the reader as to what the reply means is a reply whose identification is indicated but not given. The reader seeks a reply which maintains the meaning; hence the idea of identity, of paraphrase, of substitution that the figurative continues to evoke for the reader when he is confronted with the literal. "It is one o'clock" means figuratively "Let's go eat" for the listener who asks himself the question for which the first sentence can be a reply, and who finds the second a reply to the same question. The opposition between literal and figurative obliges him to play an active role, since he is explicitly interrogated by what the sentence says, for which he cannot accept the literal meaning. When he seeks the meaning, the listener questions that which is under questioning in what is said. The literal and the figurative are the stages of articulation of the problematological difference.

The above is easily explained by what I call the "law of complementarity." If one speaks or writes, it is because one has a question in mind. Using language is how one responds to it. The problem itself remains implicit, because it is assumed to be known by the mere fact of reply, by the answer as such, or by what is previous to it. The question-response difference articulates itself here in the implicit-explicit. This problematological difference must be stressed in another way if the problem is to be communicated in order to be resolved, that is, if the resolution depends on the interlocutor. Form will play the role of problematological differentiator: a declarative form for the reply, and a nondeclarative one to indicate what the problem is. This type of codification implies that the context does not permit us to differentiate what is problematical from what is not. If the context provides enough information to differentiate, then form can free itself from the demand of problematological differentiation to a higher degree. The richer the context, the more form will deliteralize itself, the context serving as a problematological and figurative mediator. The less the context is able to be invoked, the greater the grammaticalization of the meaning (that is, of the problematic) will be. There is thus semantico-hermeneutic complementarity between form and context.

Fiction is characterized by the formalization of its own context. Let us call this concern for verisimilitude, which may be as weak as one can imagine, "auto-contextualization." Clearly this means the integration of the problematological difference into the text itself. This difference always provides the form of the figurative meaning of the text.

What becomes of the law of complementarity at the level of auto-contextualization, at the level of the literary? The more a problem is enunciated as such in the text, perforce the more literal it is. We have thus an explicit resolution in the text itself—the problematological difference is the implicit, figurative, which assures the unity of the text. Detective stories and love stories come to mind.

The less a problem is stated, i.e., the less it is made literal, the more the form is made problematical. There is figuration in the text itself through its arrangement, its style, and by recourse to the enigmatic usage of the poetic form. And the more a text is enigmatic, the more the answer that it enunciates will have as an object the fact that it is problematic, referring itself thus to its own problematizing, dereferentialized structure. The deconstruction, the intertextuality, the denoted connotation, the withdrawal of the mimetic, all of these emerge as the effect of the demand of problematological differentiation.

In daily usage the context allows forms to mean something other than what is literally said, that is, to suggest, to evoke; hence, quite simply, to question. In literature we have a fictionalization of the context, therefore, figuration, textualization of the problematological difference. The figuration is minimal when the text attempts to reproduce reality; hence, a problematization of the real which is the referent of the explicit. Increasing figuration occurs as the problem becomes less explicit. Form must then emphasize the problematic by becoming more enigmatic. The minimal degree of figurativeness is the textuality itself, which does not signify anything other than that the problematological difference is implicit in the production and the reading of the text as to its meaning, a meaning not literally said but rendered by the ordering of the textual components and their formalization in general into a textual unit.

This leads us to conclude that there is unity to the rhetorical field. It is characterized by the resolution of its problems. Contradictory argumentation, logical reasoning, and literary expression are the modalities of this problematological articulation. It is due to an extremely restrictive conception of inference that the radical separation of these modalities has been sustained. Can one, therefore, be surprised at the exclusion of

fictional rhetoric and of the subordination of argumentation to a propositionalized logic? It is the natural consequence of inference conceived on
purely propositionalist grounds.

4. FROM PROPOSITIONAL INFERENCE TO PROBLEMATOLOGICAL INFERENCE

Aristotle defines inference as a discourse in which, something being
stated, something other follows from it (*Prior Analytics,* I, 1, 24b18).
Such a definition, however classical, seemed self-evident to its author. By
this "evidence" Aristotle encrusted inference in a propositionalist version
which has lasted two thousand years, and thus impeded a broadening
concept of inference from expressing that which constitutes its reality.
Nonetheless, Aristotle's definition has played an essential historic role,
although it has been a most restrictive one, and least satisfying in the
codification, condemned though unsurpassed by Descartes and J. S. Mill.

What does this vision of inference presuppose? Why must there be
otherness (i.e., a difference) in order for there to be deductive inference? The answer cannot be found in syllogistic theory itself. It only
stipulates that deduction would be invalid if this difference were not
respected. It begs the question to solve it. If one says that the premise
according to Aristotle, is that which is asked "for verification," one will
understand that the difference to be respected is the problematological
difference, however denied because it is propositionalized. Within
propositionalism the imperative of the problematological difference,
though embodied, is not justified. Aristotle, then, only invokes the consequences of its violation: circularity. What is circularity? It is the fact of
supposing a problem already resolved at the level of its very expression,
of considering as an answer that which is precisely under questioning (I
call it problematological indifference), thus rendering the question a
purely rhetorical one (the only function of questioning since Plato and
Aristotle). But keeping the problems and solutions distinct is not a propositional virtue. In fact, propositionalism can account for such a requirement only by the notion of the use or efficacy of the reasoning. It is
rather a problematological virtue, a question-answer relation, and not a
relation between propositions.

Inference is thus a question-answer relation; there is inference every
time one can pass from one to the other. Inference is then a problematological notion. It includes propositional inference, which thus

loses its monopoly. Propositional inference links the assertoric expression of a question to that of its answer, both of which are considered from the assertoric point of view. This is always possible if one wants to separate assertability from its base.

The consequences of our approach are essential. Inference is no longer only deductive, since any passage from a question to its answer constitutes an inference. In order for there to be inference it is sufficient to arrive at an answer while making explicit the passage from the question. An answer that states the question that it expresses, and that resolves it because its object is to express it, as in philosophy, is a problematological deduction. Kant's transcendental deduction is a good example. An answer that is constructed with a middle term that links it to the question is also an inference, in this case a syllogism. There is a syllogism when the question cannot be resolved from its own thematization. This means that something other than the question is needed in order to arrive at its answer. The Greeks also called this synthesis, since the decomposition of the problematic is not enough. For us it is only one particular type of inference, even if historically it was adopted for the reasons we have seen as the norm, thus excluding argumentative inference, philosophical inference, and problematological inference, as well as figurative, contextual, and literary implication, without speaking of induction, which has remained paradoxical since Hume.

4

Reasoning with Language

1. WHY LANGUAGE?

Recourse to language is inscribed in the general framework of human action. Men act in terms of the problems which are posed to them and which they themselves must face because those problems define human existence. Therefore, language contributes to the resolution of our problems. There are only two ways of confronting a problem with the aid of language: either one expresses the problem because its resolution depends upon another person, or one gives the solution to another person who is interested in the question or who has become interested because the question is being treated. We easily comprehend that language can be used, in the first case, directly to induce what one should believe and, in the second, indirectly to incite one to take a stance on the question by suggesting to the audience the conclusion to be drawn, i.e., the answer to infer and the correlative choices to be ultimately adopted as action. We shall return to that double possibility later.

2. THE TWO MAJOR CATEGORIES OF FORMS

This double function of language is decisive in employing forms. If one says what one thinks of a question, in other words, if one states the solution to the question, the form used will be declarative. Since the difference between questions and answers conceived as the difference between problems and solutions is the constitutive difference of language, this difference must necessarily be formally marked. Thus, when one does not declare a solution but expresses a problem, one has natural recourse to a nondeclarative form that specifies for the interlocutor the problem which one expects him to resolve.

Take several examples:

(1) It is nice outside.
(2) Close the door!
(3) What time is it?
(4) I would like to know whether you are coming tomorrow.
(5) Is he not dishonest?

In (1), the problem of the weather is evoked by the speaker, who propounds his opinion concerning the question. The proposition responds to a question which is implied as the theme of conversation: what is in question is the weather. In (2) and (3), the speaker manifests his problem and makes it known explicitly to obtain the solution. The expression of the problem in (2), which is to see a certain door closed by a certain person, therefore to be obeyed, is not declarative. In (1), the solution is declared, but the problem is not because of the exigency to respect the difference between a question and an answer. In (2), the problem must be explicitly posed; therefore, by virtue of this same difference, the solution is not declared. The same reasoning applies to (3).

We can formulate the following general law: given that the fundamental unit of language is the question-answer pair, the use of language is always situated and defined as a function of this pair. The consequences of this law are by now well known:

1. All use of language responds to a certain problem, even when the point is to express the problem
2. If the object of any resolution is to present a response, the problem which has induced that response no longer exists once the response is offered. Therefore, the object of language is not to express problems, but to express solutions. The result is an opposition between

solution and problem which corresponds to that between the explicit and the implicit. A problem is not affirmed even when it is made manifest; i.e., it is not declared, it is posed

3. To answer through language, to call upon the explicit to treat a certain problem, is to give form to it. The form marks the difference between problems and solutions *qua* language; the form distinguishes between problems and solutions according to the line of demarcation between the implicit (the unformed) and the explicit (the formed)

4. When we respond to a problem by expressing it, this partial resolution, which calls forth a complementary resolution, is formally marked as a partial resolution. This *non-dit* (unexpressed) of the whole problem reminds one of the "life-forms" so dear to Wittgenstein, to which correspond diverse uses of language which nonetheless never exhaust them[1]

Obviously, it still must be shown that the form is not the only way to mark the difference between questions and answers. Examples (4) and (5) clearly show this difference; (4) expresses a question in the declarative mode, and (5) is a hidden affirmation that the "he" in question is dishonest. If you doubt this affirmation, experiment by asking your boss if he is dishonest. You will see by his reactions whether he considers your phrase a question or an assertion.

3. THE EPISTEMIC TRANSLATION OF QUESTIONS

Many questions can be translated by the general formulation: the question X is about knowing *whether* X (or *what, when, why, where*... X). For example,

(6) When is he coming?

can be translated by "The question is *to know when* he comes";

(7) Is it nice outside this morning?

can be translated by this epistemic formulation: "The question is to know whether it is nice outside this morning."

The interrogative *whether* characterizes questions for which the totality of answers can be reduced to an alternative. This interrogative *whether* can be found again in the general formulation of the question seen epistemically. ("What constitutes the question X, namely X, is the question of knowing *whether* X." "The arrival of John constitutes the question" is equivalent to "The question is to know whether John is arriving.") Such a translating of a question does not always work: "Would you please pass the salt?" is not a question of knowing whether you are willing to do so or not. This alternative addresses a problem to be solved by some action rather than by some linguistic response. What is left rhetorically open is the addressee's decision to act or not.

4. THE AUTONOMIZATION OF THE SPOKEN AND THE WRITTEN

The answer, as an apocritico-problematological unit, defines at least two questions, and because of it the dialogical possibility of language is grounded at the same time as the autonomization of answers in relation to the questions from which they originate.

To refer to the problematological is to consider any discourse in reference to the problems from which it derives. It is, consequently, to consider it as an answer. But does not such a consideration pertain to the apocritical? The problematological, broadly conceived as any reference to questions, seems to encompass the apocritical as a particular case. But the contradiction is only an apparent one. Problematologically speaking, an answer, as answer, refers to some question as answer, i.e., emerges as apocritical with respect to that particular question. Reference to questions only occurs when answers are stipulated as such. But generally, the problematological dimension of discursivity, which implies the underlining of its apocritical relation through the differentiating shadows of the questions involved, vanishes into the apocritical, which is meant not to appear as such.

The solution for a certain question no longer refers to it, and its character of solution does not explicitly appear; hence, the illusion of autonomy of discourse in relation to problems. The problematological dimension of the answer necessarily implies an apocritical one, since an answer resolves some question or other. The problematological reference of the answer can only indicate the presence of another question. This other question is different from the one solved by the answer *qua* answer for fear of duplicating its primary apocritical character, when some question other than the one primarily solved is under consideration. Those two questions must remain different by belonging, for instance, to another questioning process. But, then, it can at most contribute to some resolution by expressing another question to which it is not the solution.

Discourse being apocritical and problematological does not imply that it will find another question to express once it has solved a first one. There must necessarily be a mediation through which what was unquestioned is made problematic. Two notions are in play here: the problematic (vs. the problematological) and the mediation that brings it forth. The actualization of the problematological is the problematic; to make problematic an assertion which was only an answer and which potentially posed a question is a matter of context. The context is the mediator of the problematological difference, the means by which a difference between what is the question and what is the answer is established effectively, i.e., actualized *hic et nunc*. Because what constitutes an answer to a given problem cannot be a question for the same locutor who has resolved the question by his proposed answer, the context necessarily involves at least two questioners: one for whom the answer is only an answer, the other for whom it constitutes a problem. The answer is not the answer, inasmuch as it continues to constitute a question, either by not resolving the question it was intended to resolve or by eliciting one or several other questions that it would express or help to resolve. In all cases, because the first answer contains a question it calls for a second answer, an answer that can range from silence, approval, or disinterest to rejection pure and simple.[2]

In any case, the context is the mediator through which the difference between question and answer is actualized at the level of produced answers. The context is a necessary mediator which counterbalances the autonomization of discourse with respect to the problems that have engendered it. The realization of that autonomy is therefore conditioned by the context in inverse proportion to the amount of given information.

The contextualization of the problematological difference enables the agents of discourse, for example, to see an assertion behind an interrogative phrase and vice versa (see examples [4] and [5], respectively). In general, the problematological difference is more extensively marked by form as the context becomes less informative in the mind of the locutor for the listener. The difference must be marked less extensively by form if the context allows the listener to differentiate the locutor's problems from his solutions. An interlocutor who knows what the locutor of X thinks will know that (5) is covert affirmation of that opinion of X. *In abstracto,* (5) can be considered just as much an authentic request for information as an insinuation.

In science, the context has a reduced role; explanations are put forth in a particular way adapted to the audience. Context, however, is annulled in theoretical constructions. As a consequence, the bringing forth to form is determining to such an extent that formalization appears to the scientists as an assurance of optimal scientificity, i.e., of decontextualization, which also means objectivity.

5. THE PROPOSITION AS PROPOSITION OF AN ANSWER: A NEW THEORY OF REFERENCE

The consequence of the apocritico-problematological unity of discursivity is clear: discursivity must contain within itself its own duality. How does it succeed?

(8) Napoleon is the winner of the battle of Austerlitz

seems to be an example of pure apocritical statement without any problematological element, while the reverse applies to example (7). In fact, any statement can be problematologically analyzed. The description in (8) specifies that Napoleon is the one who is the winner of the battle of Austerlitz; the "who" refers explicitly to that "who" which is in question in the statement and specifies the meaning one must get from "Napoleon." This problematological analysis, which bares the interrogative structure of the assertion, can be extended to all the terms in it: Is not "Austerlitz," for example, the place *which*... or *that*... —and so on until the addressee is satisfied and finally understands what was in question in the statement, i.e., what the statement signified. In the same way, one can emphasize the apocritical structure of discourse precisely by suppressing all the interrogative clauses and substituting a declaration for it, a proposition. Phrase (7) states something, in this case that the locutor in question (i.e., the one who is referred to as so and so) is asking whether it is nice outside this morning. Example (2) states indirectly that the locutor wishes to see the door closed by the addressee. By saying that much explicitly this time, one not only conveys the meaning of (2) and (7) but also suppresses any interrogation; one leaves interrogation for what is literally out-of-the-question. This semantic equivalence results from the dual nature of discursivity, whereupon one can express (8) by an expanded version involving interrogation to indicate what is in question in (8) as not raising it any longer.

6. WHAT IS MEANING?

Meaning, said Wittgenstein, is that which responds to the question of meaning. Without doubt, there is a link between meaning and interrogation, yet understanding can occur when interrogation does not. The examples in the preceding paragraphs are revelatory; the meaning of a statement, of a proposition, of a discourse, is given once one knows what is in question. Should the subject in question be unknown, however (following Wittgenstein's advice), one finds oneself inquiring about what was not questionable, namely, what was in question in the statement or written sentence. The answer to this request for meaning explicitly stipulates this question. The meaning emerges from the interaction between two questions; it emerges as unveiling the answer as answer, i.e., by referring some assertion to the question which it treats. A nonproblematic intelligibility is an implicit (mental?) answer indicating that to which the question refers. One can always therefore develop an answer in reference to its question (i.e., the question of the answerer) through the bias of interrogatives. Indeed, through such a problematological analysis, what is in question in the statement becomes defined and the meaning of the terms captured.

What is the link between these terms and the global proposition? Why are there judgments, why are there statements, and how are they answers? Where does the unity of the proposition originate the atomic character of its irreducible complementarity of elementary terms? Aristotle thought that this complementarity pertained to the subject-predicate relation. Not until Frege did we realize that similar terms could indifferently serve as subject and as predicate, and that the relation between terms could not alone suffice to account for their complementarity to form a judgment. Aristotle's explanation, inasmuch as it claimed to account for the genesis of predication, failed to be up to the task. Frege replaced Aristotle's explanation with that of the complementarity of functions and variables. Functions are incomplete signs, concepts, which by nature are empty and need to be completed by signs which exhaust them. The articulation of names and of predicates thus produces judgments. Predicates have a reference and so too have names, concepts, and objects, respectively. Together, they form judgments which too have reference. The difference (and, therefore, their complementarity) cannot rest on the fact that they are referring expressions, but on what they denote. *Bedeutung* means *reference:* denotation but also signification. An extensional version of meaning is bound to lead to the conflation of reference and meaning. That conflation is why Frege distinguishes *Sinn* (sense, or meaning) from the corresponding reference. Signification emerges, then, as a relation between some *Sinn* and some *Bedeutung:* the meaning [*Sinn*] of a judgment differs from its signification (*Sinn* + *Bedeutung*].

Beyond the numerous difficulties raised by such a concept, what remains entirely unexplained is why there is reference in language, why it has a major role when the meaning or the signification of propositions must be given, and why judgments should be seen as autonomous entities based on complementary parts.

I contend that only a theory of questioning can successfully face all these queries. Indeed, reference is precisely what is covered by an interrogative in a proposition and can always be defined as such. One can easily verify that fact by returning to example (8) and its development. Since one can approach all terms with the help of interrogatives, one is necessarily led to ascribe a reference to them. A negative answer to what is covered by something said can then imply a lack of reference. Reference, in fact, is attributed through a process (one speaks of *judgments* when one should use the word *judging*) through which interrogatives disappear. The questions vanish in the solution treating them, i.e., treating them as having been problematic. But they leave traces. What Napoleon is obscures what is denoted by "Napoleon," and goes without saying; the expression "to be the winner of Austerlitz" is understood once we know what Austerlitz is and what it is to win a battle.

The answer to these questions generates a judgment in which what was in question at the outset disappears as such; the interrogatives are suppressed in the dynamic of judging (and thinking) to form example (8). An interrogative, however, can be introduced again to expand (8): "*Who* is Napoleon?" or "*Who* won at Austerlitz?" for instance. What is in question can always reappear as being solved if necessary for explicit understanding and explication. Hence the use of relative clauses that define terms specifies what should be understood by them; i.e., their what-ness, their reference, and their meaning become here identical. Judgments result from the necessity of answering, i.e., of not making problematic expressions which are treated as having been in question.

The term being made problematic can be defined (at any rate, can be characterized or determined) by the answer to the expression of its problematological nature. Such an answer is explicitly posed as such when, for example, one says, instead of "Napoleon is the winner of Austerlitz," "Napoleon is the one who . . ." The reference to what is in question here is explicit. But clearly this amounts to the same thing in both cases of assertorical stipulation. Consequently, reference is an essential feature of language because language arises from the interrogative relation between man and reality, and because to judge is to respond to an interrogation. We thus see why names and predicates have a referent, as well as how both merge into judgments.[3]

What is in question in an answer (i.e., its meaning or what it treats) and the terms it involves are distinct. Is the Napoleon in question what is in question in "Napoleon is the winner of the battle of Austerlitz?" Is Frege's principle of composition—the reference or the signification of a judgment depends on the reference of its constituent parts—always valid? Clearly not. The person in question in "Napoleon is the winner of Austerlitz" is not what is in question, undoubtedly because what he is does not directly come into question, even if there is question of Napoleon in the sentence. That seriously limits Frege's principle of composition according to which we must look for the meaning of terms, therefore of words, and not of discourse or of propositions, isolated or not.

In general, an answer which treats a certain question refers to it, but not in the way "Napoleon" refers to *Napoleon* as an object of historical reality. Hence, nonreferential (conceived traditionally) discourse (literature, for example) can be endowed with meaning. An "object" (if we must use this hackneyed term) is only apprehendable at the end of a judging process which characterizes it as such. To return to our example: Napoleon is the winner of Austerlitz. I do not know who this man is. His name means nothing to me. The person in question will only become known to me if he ceases to constitute a question. The answer "He is the one *who* won at Austerlitz" no longer suffices; a substitute is needed that can involve a correct but familiar characterization. Napoleon will be what answers this description. While the object is that upon which the answer bears, and while the answer thereby guarantees its independence, the answer is only real and knowable through the answer which suppresses it as a question for me. (See again the discussion in note 3 of this chapter.)

The problem is identical with what is problematic. If I speak of the problem of the victory at Austerlitz, this victory itself is in question; I am speaking of nothing but that and what really is the problem to discuss—the victory at Austerlitz. What is problematic is not the solution and yet the solution bears upon it. This "upon" marks the distance between knowing and the known, i.e., its independence relative to the answers that describe the known. Since a problem is identifiable with what is problematic, the answer must refer to what was problematic though being different, since the problematological difference must be respected. Distance occurs, and this act bears our dynamic relation to the world (referentiality) as different and external. The "object" does not answer, but an answer is made based upon it. It is mute, but we make it speak. How carefully we must understand expressions such as "the dialogue with nature" in order to refer to the interrogation of reality; this "of" summarizes the distance.

The methodological consequence one must draw is that one cannot ask any indifferent question when one wants to explore the real scientifically. For scientific interrogation to be conclusive, it can only be expressed as a single alternative. If I ask "What are you doing tomorrow?" I am introducing many possible answers, and my interlocutor selects one. But nature does not answer. However, if I ask "Are you doing this or that tomorrow?" or "You are doing that tomorrow, aren't you?" I am asking my interlocutor to confirm a proposition or to deny it. I know as a consequence what he is doing tomorrow if the answer is positive. This latter interrogation is the one I can address to nature. There being no answer from nature, I must propose a solution to nature, or, more accurately, a solution is likely to be confirmed or denied by my experimentation or observation upon nature. Still, things are not always so simple as they may seem, because one does not necessarily draw from one's relation to nature a pure validation or invalidation; the proposition or solution is only more or less confirmed by facts without being completely confirmed once and for all.

The only type of questions where a proposition confronts its own negation is the one that presents only one alternative, yes or no. The logical process by which one reaches that answer is traditionally called analysis, because analysis considers the proposition, as given, to be justified; transforms into a "solution" what is problematic; and, rejecting the negation of the solution, succeeds in saying that this solution is the true one. Such a process, going from a problem to its solution by a simple formal conversion of the interrogative into the assertorical, implies a certain type of problem, i.e., one that can be simply solved by yes or no—a single alternative. At the end of the analysis, the validity of the proposition has been established or not. If such is not the case, the contradictory statement becomes the valid answer; the latter is then obtained whatever happens.

Scientific interrogation is essentially the quest for justification. Some answer is proposed, and one simply requires a yes or no about it that justifies some choice offered, although obtaining the yes or no is often not very easy, even indirectly. The questions formulated involve alternatives for which accommodation is reached and in some manner decided upon by recourse to experience. The quest for meaning would be misled if it were modeled on scientific research. Meaning is neither the answer nor the question but the link between question and answer. The problem to be resolved gives meaning to the solution that it would not have *per se*. Thus, one can say of a statement that this or that is in question to clarify the meaning of that statement. Interlocutors who know how to make themselves understood do not say "The meaning is . . ."; they say what they have to say.

Judgments, then, mean something by what they declare, i.e., by denoting something. Referentiality is a by-product of answerhood. The relation between question and answer, although immanent in the answer, remains implicit. The answer says something (what it affirms is in the foreground) other than itself, because the goal of questioning process is not to express itself but to express something else. The goal of the ensuing answer is not to refer to the questions that have generated it; it is not to designate itself as answer, i.e., as being its own reference, but to say something else. The answerhood of the answer realizes itself in repressing its being an answer, i.e., by referring to something else in question. The answer includes the capacity to treat what is under question, and this is what denotes an effective reference outside itself. It can only point to the reference. The answer says what it says without saying that it says it: that it is an answer. The nature of an answer is not to assert itself (as answer) but to say something; it says what the question is, but does not say it is a question.

Having an answer to the question means the problem is no longer under question *qua* question. The question manifests itself as the absence which underlies any discourse. If my problem, for example, is to know what you are doing tomorrow, the assertion "I am going to town" answers it. I do not expect you to say "The assertion 'I am going to town' answers your question" because the fact that this statement is presented as an answer and preserves the meaning of the answer does not in any way imply that you are going to town; information about that action was precisely the purpose of my interrogation and not the stipulation of some statement about that information.

Because the goal of answers is not to be offered as such, the essential property of linguistic signs is to refer to something other than themselves. A familiar definition indeed. We know, of course, that paradoxes emerge the moment one tries to make a set of propositions systematically self-referential. Nonetheless, one answer can speak for another just as well as it can express a question. There are apocritical answers and problematological answers. I have emphasized elsewhere that this distinction preserves the problematological difference, to the extent that they both incorporate the difference into their answerhood.[4]

In the actual use of language, one knows what is under question; thus one need not mention it. The answer does not say itself. The discovery of meaning proceeds from the context and from the information it contains for the audience. The audience functions as the implicit questioner. It considers the spoken or the written as answer; the question treated therein summons the attention of the audience in one way or another (if only to provoke signs of disinterest). The audience is questioning, and question it does because an answer is being propounded to it. An answer to what, for what, on what?

The meaning of an answer is its link to a specific question. If the meaning is a problem for the addressee of the answer, the problem will have to be resolved by offering an answer which duplicates the initial one, in that it emphasizes the apocritical nature of initial answer. The meaning of a given statement is what it says, and this interrogative "what" sufficiently shows that the question of meaning is implicit in what is said to unveil itself as what is said. There is a duplication process in the explication of meaning, since it repeats what is said in being explicitly referred to as what is covered by the interrogative and is maintained in the answer as introducing an answer. The reference to the locutor's question is explicit in the explicit request for meaning. The signifying answer is certainly equivalent to the signified answer in that both reply to the same question. For example, "John is single" is equivalent to "John is not married"; if the first statement answers question Q in context C, it is likely that the second will also.

This equivalence is not always automatic, because one cannot affirm that two sentences are semantically equivalent without referring them to what they answer respectively in some given context. If the problem, for instance, is "Make a sentence in three words," both statements can no longer be exchanged as equivalent. They are not answers to that question. The meaning of the first statement is not the same as in the second, because the point is to produce a whole in three words. The meaning of the statement depends not on the statement alone but on the question to which it must correspond. This meaning pertains to its nature as answer, which presupposes a definite question on which this statement depends;

an equivalent answer assumes equivalence in relation to this same question. Hence, "John is single" may have the same meaning as "Albert is short," with respect to the question of having a three-word sentence. That equivalence can explain that some onomatopoeia, for instance, can mean "I despise you" or "Go to hell" for the addressee in certain contexts.

An answer which gives the meaning differs from the one that has a meaning stipulated by it, even if only by means of what they both actually reply to. Indeed, the answer with meaning takes this meaning in relation to a repressed question (*non-dit*). It resolves the *non-dit,* and the question which is no longer a question appears in the answer as having been resolved by it. The answer does not express itself as answer (that would still be indicating the question as present when it actually is absent). The answer therefore does not say itself, but it says something else. Nevertheless, the answer treats a definite question by what it says while it does not say "This is the question raised . . ."; neither does it say "This is the answer."

The presence of a question implicit to the spoken (identified thereby as answer) demonstrates that in some internal manner it has a meaning.

This meaning can, of course, elude the questioner confronted by it. The answer he is looking for will duplicate the answer he does not understand, but he does not understand because he does not see what it answers. The question eludes him, and the goal of the answer to his hermeneutic interrogation is to discover the question that he deems to be absent from the explicit. For instance, if an interlocutor does not understand example (2), the initial locutor will reply simply "I want you to do *this* or *that,*" rather than "My problem is . . . ," the first answer being more or less rich in information, and the this or that specified, according to the degree of the interlocutor's misunderstanding. This answer is similar in meaning to "Close the door." Its meaning differs from "Close the door" in that the second answer is not the one which the locutor would have provided from the start, assuming that the addressee could understand it. This answer is an answer to the question of meaning, and the second question, not being the locutor's, is apocritically marked. It comes forth as answer since the addressee was asking (himself) about the meaning of another answer. As an answer, it is apocritical and then declarative, even if it asserts what the locutor meant to say, i.e., his problem.

Therefore, semantically equivalent answers differ in that they reply to different questions. The identity of their propositional content derives from the fact that the answer which specifies the meaning of an answer expresses what was in question without it being expressed as such. The

question treated in an answer appears in it, but not explicitly. The answer is the answer about something—the question—and not the question itself. Because meaning is the link between question and answer, no
linguistic transaction can be devoid of signification, an immanent signification. It may, however, sound problematic for the one who did not
initiate the discourse. That the locutor presupposes in (2) which door is
in question (i.e., the point of the question), or which action is to be
performed in this case, shows that the meaning of those terms is referential only to the extent that the explication of their meaning or even the
presupposition of their having meaning is intelligible only as questioning. Something must answer those names, and the predicates as well, and
this answering gives them meaning. The ensuing answer brings together
a potentially interrogative clause and what it denotes. Of course, the
answering can arise from an interrogation which does not bear on the
meaning of the terms of the answer. This is not the general purpose of
interrogation, but there would be no judgment at all without some
previous need: the need to suppress what is under question as a question, to answer what was under question by presenting it as no longer in
question.

7. MEANING AS THE LOCUS OF DIALECTIC

Any discourse is the source of dialogue because of its problematological
nature. Apocritical for the locutor, it is no longer under question. When
discourse is problematological, it can only be so for other locutors.
When it is an answer, it is also a question; but for whom? If an answer
raises a question, it becomes problematic again; the question raised is a
revived one. Considering the indeterminant character of making effective problematics, the proposed answer is directed to everyone; in this
directing we must see the basis of Perelman's famous concept of the
universal audience.

Meaning is precisely the medium through which an answer is taken
over by someone other than the one who proposed it. The addressee takes
responsibility, though perhaps only provisionally, for an answer which is
not his, i.e., a problematic that belongs to the original locutor. Hence the
metaphor "to put oneself in the place of the other" indicates that one
understands him or, in some cases, manipulates him. Again the signification is redundant with what it signifies. The point is to grasp clearly what
is under question before one pronounces on it, either in a concordant

sense indicated by the locutor or in a contrary sense. Taking over someone else's interrogation is erroneously described when one assimilates it
with a *post facto* reenactment of his mental behavior. In fact, the question
is indicated by the answer, and therefore to proceed to the original interrogation as the locutor did in the first place is unnecessary.

A discourse raises, evokes, suggests, or indicates a question. The addressee behaves dually toward the question. Confronted with the answer,
he must necessarily confront the question. The answer is under question
for him because, even if he completely and implicitly adheres to it, he
does so only because the answer resolves a question in the circumstances
that he is wondering about or that previously interested him. An answer is
a proposition, and to make it problematic amounts to enclosing it in the
alternative which makes its negation possible. The question would not
arise otherwise. Such question-posing obliges him to take a stance on the
question. He is called upon to answer. We know the risks of such a summons upon him. The addressee-questioner may not have thought of the
question; the question can put him directly into question by its content
(the "burning question"); it can emphasize a disagreement about what
must be thought of it, etc. This is no doubt where one must look for the
origin of hollow, conventional politeness and social manners in general, as
well as for inceptions of conversation like "How are you?" or "Hello." Such
conversation is innocent in that it does not raise for the addressee any
question prone to produce an answer in contradiction to the answers to
his own most personal problems.

All this also accounts for the importance of dialectical strategies; the
initial questioner proposes an answer knowing that the addressee thinks
this or that about the question. He adapts accordingly to convey his
answer, for the addressee to feel, rightly or wrongly, that the answer also
replies to his questions. With no clue about such questions in cases
where the audience is large and indeterminate, prudence is necessary
and the terms will be more shadowy. What they cover over will more or
less be left in the dark. Politics has been successful in perverting the will
of the endeavor to convince, so much so that this endeavor itself has
come to be spurned.

8. ARGUMENTATION

Argumentation is often defined as the endeavor to convince. The argumentative dimension is essential to language in that any discourse tries to

persuade the person it addresses. Argumentation, however, is also characterized as nonformal, nonconstraining reasoning, in opposition to logical
reasoning, which is characterized by rigorous necessity without the possibility of appeal. Both definitions are related; one only argues because
reasons do not follow upon each other with the absolute necessity of
mathematics, leaving room for possible disagreement. Nevertheless,
mathematical demonstration is likewise addressed to someone it is trying
to persuade. One should, by the way, examine why demonstration is
convincing in itself; nothing actually prevents anyone from refusing his
assent to mathematical truths. Should one perhaps conceive of demonstration as a mode of argumentation? On the other hand, there can be argumentation, i.e., a nonformal combination of propositions, without persuasion coming into account. The two previous definitions do not coincide.
Furthermore, if all discourse is persuasive—therefore argumentative—
how is one justified in opposing argumentation to formal reasoning,
which is discourse just as well?

In reality, this opposition derives from the fact that in formal languages
no possibility is left for contradictory propositions in the system. No
alternative, therefore no possible questioning, is allowed that does not
lead to the answers offered by the formal system. Mathematical demonstration is convincing because it states the answer to a given question; if
one wonders about this question, one must accept that answer, hence,
agreement and adhesion to the answer. Nonformal reasoning offers no
guarantee that the question raised will not remain open in the absence
of a constraining process of resolution. Hence, the possibility for the
alternative remains open and the chance for possible contradiction
arises.

Consequently, argumentation pertains to the theory of questioning.
What is an argument but an opinion on a question? To raise a question,
which is the essence of discourse, is to argue. The question being
posed—the possibility of an opposed opinion, or a debate—is posed
along with it. But what question are we referring to? If a question must
be faced in a given context, the argument is the answer which occurs as
a conclusion on the question. Contrary to mathematics, the premises
and rules of progression remain implicit in the context: they are not
under question. The progress from question to answer is an actual inference via the context and the information it provides. Inversely, the
addressee is a questioner who goes back to the question raised in the
answer, inferring the former from the latter via the context. This inference is not constraining, because it does not relate to assertions posed as
such, in such a way that the second would be imposed upon the ad-

dressee by the necessity of this relation. On the contrary, a flexible inference does not require being rendered totally explicit, and its conclusion appears as a simple possibility in the way any answer is *a priori* with respect to an *a priori* question. In the end, "It is going to rain" is only a possible answer with respect to the question of what the weather will be like tomorrow.

One can generalize: there is argumentation the moment the explicit and the implicit are related. Inference occurs at the level of the utterance itself. By the question it raises, evokes, suggests, implies, or "implicates" (Paul Grice), the act of speech concludes in favor of a solution to the question treated; it serves as an argument in a *pro* and *contra.* Argumentation functions as the demand for a conclusion, possibly of a certain decision (by direct or indirect persuasion) with respect to the problem posed in the context where it occurs. Such a context provides the protagonists with the informative resources which are necessary for the inference of the answer-conclusion. Shared by the locutor and the addressee, these pieces of information can remain implicit, contrary to what takes place in mathematics or in the experimental sciences, where the scientist does not know who he is addressing or what his interlocutor already knows or thinks. Because this relation between protagonists rests upon putative knowledge, upon knowledge of knowledge, upon hypotheses formulated about the problem of the Other, because the progress from a problem to a solution is rooted in a context wherein it is posed, because any solution remains problematological no matter what, nothing guarantees that the solution will be accepted as expected by the person proposing it. Far from resolving a question by stipulating what he thinks of it, the locutor can generate a debate from the moment that he has thought he had closed it.

I said earlier that an argument evokes (suggests, implies, etc.) a question. This question may barely preoccupy the addressee. However, contrary to scientific discourse, which is peremptory in that it does not call for an answer, ordinary language always envisions one or more specific questioners whose personal problematic is taken into account by the locutor. If the locutor does not, he runs an even chance of displeasing or not interesting the questioners. One can, of course, raise a question which the addressee has not previously considered. If, however, the questioner addressed is ignored by the locutor, the locutor appears to be the only protagonist that matters. He talks to himself, or, as is the case in science, he acts as if the personal problematics of the people he is addressing do not count. The practice of monologue with someone else presupposes that a hierarchical relation is in force, a distribution of power which compels listening or other types of deviation related to an inflated ego.

Argumentation refers to the possibility of making problematic the answers given, to the extent that to say what one thinks about a question is not enough to make this declaration into an argumentation. Argumentation presupposes inference, i.e., more than one statement directly answering one question. The locutor has both the question and the answer. Only the hearer proceeds to an inference; by suggesting the latter, though, one can also say that the locutor resorts to argumentation by offering one argument. For the audience, there is an argument since it must infer the adequacy of the answer; hence, the communication of the answer is only argumentative, in the mind of the locutor, if someone other than himself correlates them. The locutor has an argument concerning some question when he answers it, but he does not, therefore, proceed to an argumentation. Argumentation is a direct inducing process, i.e., *direct* when the point is to induce someone to make a pronouncement or to convince him to adopt a course of conduct toward a problem, but *indirect* when one does no more than impart certain opinions or conclusions to be used later when he must face the question. In that sense, education is argumentative. Or so it should be.

9. LITERAL AND FIGURATIVE MEANING: THE ORIGIN OF MESSAGES "BETWEEN THE LINES," SUGGESTIONS, AND OTHER IMPLICIT CONCLUSIONS

The explicit is an apocritical and problematological answer. The users of language know it well through the experience they have of it. Instead of simply stating the answer to a question which one is considering, one can just as well ask a question, leaving it up to the interlocutor to make out which answer to formulate. Question (5) is a good example of this strategy. The locutor may not want or dare to say of X that he is dishonest. He may decline the responsibility for having proffered such an accusation although he really believes X is dishonest. He is asking for his interlocutor's opinion, the question being rhetorical in that the locutor has the answer (from his own point of view, at any rate). The question is real in that he is soliciting an opinion on the question even though he is suggesting this opinion by simply formulating the question. This opinion is implied between the lines; it is the figurative meaning of (5), the question being literally interrogative and not assertorical.

In the same way as there are questions which imply assertions assumed to be true from the beginning, there are answers which raise questions as hidden primary or secondary messages which give them their true meaning. Such answers deal with questions that are not the ones they apparently resolve. If I tell someone who acted foolishly, and who knows it, "That's clever!" I signify the contrary to him (i.e., irony). Since the answer is not an answer to the question raised, I am forcing my interlocutor to consider an alternative in question.

Another example: if I say "It is nice outside" as in (1), I may be arguing in favor of a certain conclusion that I would like my interlocutor to draw. I may mean "Let's go for a walk," "Let's change the subject," "Hello," or any number of other things that the context permits to be inferred, at least in the locutor's mind. Therefore, there is a literal meaning which describes atmospheric conditions in (1) and an implicit figurative meaning which is to be derived from the context according to the locutor's problem. Hence, the plurality of signification to a single discourse. Here we see the secret of the fecundity and richness of great texts—namely, never to be exhausted in their own time nor thoroughly illuminated by the circumstances and problematics of their writers (just think of Plato or Proust). A sentence, a text, a book are forever the literal meaning of implicit meanings which surge forth in the light of new contexts where new questions appear to which they relentlessly offer an answer.

In the case of the duality of meaning, one is still dealing with argumentation, but the relation between the explicit and the implicit is more subtle. The implicit is not only the contextual mediator that allows inference; it is also the argument which the addressee is being induced to agree to, without having to tell him so. Playing with the problematological character of discourse, the locutor produces an answer, knowing it is a request, a request directed to the Other for another answer, a request that is immanent in the first answer. The locutor calls upon the Other to answer by presenting to him an answer which he intentionally produces as having to be made problematic by him in another sense.

Argumentation with dual meaning is characterized by the locutor producing his answer as a request even when the answer appears to be just an answer. By asking for a different answer from the addressee, the initial answer is imagined by the locutor as necessarily suggesting and evoking the figurative answer. Far from being the answer, the figurative answer is finally imposed as answer, as the *wirklich* (effective) meaning: what the locutor meant for his audience to believe. The literal answer is proposed to constitute a question for the addressee.

Such a disguise draws upon more than one arsenal. Literature, for example, uses stories where the problematics being resolved must not be taken literally, i.e., as truth. Fiction, by masking the author's problematics, derives the specific reality of its meanings from the reader's questions, up to the forgottenness of the work, which is but one way of calling it into question. The author's problems existing in daily talk appear both distorted and enriched in and through fiction. The questioner, by producing an answer which does not literally answer what he is questioning, conceals his questions. He can allow the addressee to picture them for himself, or he can conceal them extensively to let his reader's imagination play its role.

The questioner faced with an answer will effectively render it problematic if, far from being offered as a final answer, it is posed as requiring questioning, and consequently an answer. It is an answer about which the question is to know what it answers; it is then a request for meaning. But contrary to other types of answers, this type intentionally traps the questioner and moves him to infer (= argumentation) another answer. It does so by imposing itself from the start as hermeneutically resistant, while allowing a solution to be reached without being requested explicitly from the locutor.

Whether the locutor proposes an answer in the interrogative form or intentionally expresses it as an answer requiring an answer (i.e., it was ambiguous, incongruous, etc.) matters little, since he succeeds in presenting it as having to be made problematic to be fully understood, i.e., grasped as an answer. The answer is produced with emphasis on its problematological character, to the point that the addressee perceives the need to answer. Whether the answer raises a question to which the answer is not literally identical, or generates doubt for the locutor as to its ultimate nature as answer, makes no difference in that the questioner-addressee is being used according to his role to reach an inference. Thus the figurative meaning is only a particular type of inference, to the extent that all of them solicit answering from the questioner-addressee.

5

How to Give Meaning with Words

1. THE SHORTCOMINGS OF CURRENT THEORIES AND THE GOALS OF A NEW ONE

T he aim of this chapter is to elaborate a systematic conception of meaning in order to address the various questions in which meaning is involved, questions ranging from those posed by literary language to those of everyday conversation, from the analysis of logical and referential discourse to historical comprehension.

The classical conception of language and meaning which has prevailed since the time of the ancient Greeks is not an adequate one as a general view. We can call this view the propositional model because its basic unit is the judgment, the proposition; the declarative sentence, which is true or false, is its linguistic counterpart. As John Lyons remarks about Greek grammar, "The definition of the major grammatical classes, 'nouns' and 'verbs,' was made on logical grounds, i.e., as constituents of a proposition."[1] The explanation of the relationship between subject and predicate has long been a central preoccupation of grammatical study, up to (and including) Frege's codified analysis of propositional logic.

In spite of its logical extension, propositionalism proved unable to cover the spheres of discourse irreducible to logical and sentential analysis. This may explain why a hermeneutic conception of meaning has emerged, as well as rhetorical and pragmatic theories of language in literature and everyday speech. This fragmentation does not exclude some overlapping, but we can hardly affirm that a unified view of meaning has come out of this diversity of theories. Understanding a sentence was seen as intrinsically different from understanding a text, although a text is a set of sentences. But understanding fictional discourse is not reducible to the comprehension of referential expressions, though both convey meaning. All these inconsistencies betray the weaknesses and limitations of the current theories instead of proving the fragmented nature of language as such. However, from Wittgenstein until Donald Davidson, the belief in a propositional model of linguistic meaning has been widely sustained.

For this reason, a general view of meaning is needed in which propositions cease to play a key role that they obviously cannot fulfill, given the radically different problems posed by textual wholes, by the historical sciences, and by such nonlogical discourse as literature. If we are not willing to pursue this new line of inquiry, we shall have to rest content with theories adapted only to the limited realms of linguistic objects for which they have been primarily intended (namely, individual sentences), and we shall lose track of the unity of language, a unity which some philosophers have declared impossible.

The collapse of propositionalism is now a fact, attested to by the increasing number of theories which endeavor to account for nonpropositional linguistic phenomena. Speech-act theory is one well-known example, hermeneutics and rhetoric are others. Are they the representation of a scattered reality or, rather, the reflection of an increasing inability to integrate various linguistic effects in which meaning is involved in a nonpropositional way?

In this chapter I will offer some basic principles for a unified conception of language and meaning. What are the requirements we must meet, if we want a unified view?

1. A general theory of meaning must explain sentential meaning, as well as textual meaning, be it fictional or otherwise. Meaning as reference becomes a special case of this general theory; it cannot function as the paradigm case, and even less the whole of the conception in question, as Frege suggested. Semantics and hermeneutics should not be kept apart
2. A general theory of meaning must rest on *a general view of language.* The propositional elements of the theory must not exclude others. The structure of the proposition, as composed of a subject and

a predicate, should be explained in terms of the theory offered, and not be merely assumed as a starting point

3. A general theory of meaning must integrate the various contexts for meaning, such as the literal, the figurative, the written, and the conversational. This implies a conceptualization of the role of context in the determination of meaning

In other words, these three requirements amount to the erection of an integrated view of language, in which the argumentative and rhetorical structures can find their place along with a theory of judgment.

I have called the theory which answers these requirements the problematological view of meaning. It is based on the idea that language use is a response and therefore implies the presence, implicit or not, of an underlying problem in the mind of the locutor and the minds of the addressees. To problematology is opposed propositionalism, in which propositions, also called judgments, are considered as the basic units of thought and language, with exclusive attention put on truth-values and propositional connections. Inference, reading, conversation, speech-acts, contextual or rhetorical effects, all these would be reducible to some propositional content. Judgments, however, must no longer be considered the basic measure of meaning. If the meaning of a sentence is its capacity to produce its own equivalent, are we ready to affirm that the meaning of Cervantes' *Don Quixote* is its capacity to be rewritten? Such a conclusion, which would be an extension of the propositionalist theory of meaning, would lead to what I have called *The Paradox of Don Xerox*.[2] It amounts to the search for a literal meaning in literature, as we do with everday language, as if it were natural to fall back upon such an equivalent statement when meaning is at stake.

2. MEANING AND REFERENCE: THE LIMITS AND THE QUESTIONS OF THE FREGEAN CONCEPTION

If the meaning of a judgment is another statement, it is due to the sameness of reference. "John is a bachelor" means the same as "John is not married" because all bachelors are not married. If one statement is true, the other must also be true, since they refer to the same state of affairs; they have the same truth-conditions, and they can be inferred from each other as having necessarily an identical truth-value.

Such a view of meaning has several presuppositions and consequences that render it inappropriate to serve as a general theory.

In this view, meaning is a relationship of equivalence of statements based on an identical reference. It presupposes that language is referential, and unequivocally so. Terms should refer to objects beyond any possible confusion of designation. As a result, language can be formalized, since formalism rests upon the assignment of one, and only one, reference to any symbol. Natural language, in contrast, is ambiguous to the extent that most terms can receive multiple meanings; according to the situation, they refer to different objects because the nature of everyday language is to be adaptable to quasi-infinite possibilities with finite lexical means. Symbolic languages have the specific feature that their terms only denote one item, and therefore cannot possibly be equivocal; one referent, thus one meaning. Context plays no role; everything must be explicit and specified by axioms, rules of inference, and so forth. A symbolic language is a construction that nobody speaks for the obvious reason that we always use language in a given context of utterance. But Frege's contention is that we always mean something particular and precise when we resort to language. If we are intelligible to our audience, we must be capable of expressing some literal statement which is the logical form of our sentence(s). Our discourse may be equivocal and imply several readings, but if it means anything it must denote some statement held to be true and not any object, even if the context plays a role in the determination of what is precisely referred to. It is on this ground that Frege can uphold the view that he has offered a general theory of meaning.

In reality, Frege's theory suffers from too many limitations to be entitled to such a general application. Since it relies upon reference it can only apply to referential discourse. This necessarily excludes literature as a whole. Moreover, meaning is an identity relation that prevails as a literal relationship. And this only applies for noncontextual language in which there is no double meaning intended by the locutor. But many speech-acts, in fact, convey a suggested meaning in virtue of contextual effects. A third remark concerns the very propositional aspect of Frege's conceptualization. In order to produce an equivalent statement stipulating the meaning of another judgment, one cannot simply proceed on the basis of the sameness of the propositional reference. If so, a proposition such as "John is tall" would mean the same as "The grass is green," since they both refer to the same truth-value, which is the real propositional content of all propositions. Hence Frege's famous principle of compositionality: two equireferential propositions are substitutable as such if and only if their constituents are also equireferential. In our example, "John ≠ the grass" and " 'x is tall' ≠ 'x is green' " because not all x's that are tall are green. If "John is a bachelor" means the same as "John is not married," it is because John = John, and that x is a bachelor = x is not married, for any possible x's. Here we obviously have names and attributes that have the same references, thereby rendering the two judgments which contain them equivalent, one being the meaning of the other. The consequences of such a principle of compositionality are clearly damaging to the analysis of language in discourse. In order to understand discourse, do we really have to consider each sentence individually and dissect it into its constituent parts before understanding it? It is hardly plausible, at any rate, that to decompose discourse into propositions, and propositions into proper names and predicates, means to understand that very discourse as such. Does it not imply that discourse and texts cannot exist as autonomous entities and must be understood piecemeal, and only in a totally analytical manner?

More important, maybe, are the questions that Frege treats as being solved, as if their solutions were too obvious to merit discussion. Clearly the definition of meaning, according to Frege, must rest upon sameness of reference. The meaning of a judgment is another statement that has the same reference compositionally, hence globally. The fact that meaning is a referential notion is never questioned; nor is the fact that an identical reference must yield the meaning of the initial proposition. Meaning preserves reference, and an identical reference allows us to infer the meaning as a substitutable proposition to the one whose meaning is sought. If Frege explains how meaning happens to be a relation of identity on the basis of the identity of reference, he does not tell us why it must be an identity at all; moreover, he seems to take it for granted that the equation of meaning and reference is therefore universal. Why should meaning be an identity? Why should meaning be referential and reference play the key role? How do we know that two judgments have the same reference, i.e., the same meaning, if we do not understand them *first?* It seems to be necessary to know what they mean before being able to establish that they actually have the same reference. Frege's reasoning is circular: he asserts that two propositions have the same meaning when one means what the other means because they have the same reference. Why should reference, identity, and meaning be conflated in such a way? More than shown and expanded, such a view should be grounded and not merely assumed.

3. WHEN AND WHY MEANING IS REFERENTIAL

Meaning is often a matter of referential knowledge. To give the meaning of an isolated statement, for instance, amounts to producing an equivalent one, which affirms the *same* thing with other words. *Sinn* and *Bedeutung.* Whatever the integrated theory of meaning, it *must preserve* that sort of equivalence, based on the identity of reference. On the other hand, there are cases in which meaning is figurative, implied or inferred, nonliteral, and nonreferential. The question is then: When is meaning given by the reference, and when is it not? This query is in fact tantamount to the problem of knowing why meaning is referential, by virtue of which mechanism the two are correlated. Maybe there is a third variable, other than meaning and reference, which plays a role in the semantic reality and which is left unseen by Frege for reasons that we shall also have to discover, once the hidden factor has been extracted. And then we shall have to see whether this factor plays a key role in other semantic and hermeneutic situations, in which there is meaning but no reference. These new situations enable us to verify the hypothesis of the theory and also to generalize it by bridging the gap between texts or discourses and sentences taken as such. A general theory would then include phenomena deemed to be conceptualized only by different and often incompatible theories of language meaning.

Let us now start our analysis by considering a very simple example. Meaning here is clearly given by the truth-conditions of the sentence, in which it lends itself to a Fregean characterization.

(1) Napoleon lost at Waterloo.

I grasp the meaning of (1) if, and only if, I know who Napoleon is (what the term *Napoleon* is referring to), what losing is, and where, or what, Waterloo is. All these answers provide the references of the terms involved in (1). Frege's principle of compositionality seems to apply perfectly in this case. In fact, I can always substitute an equireferential term to any of these, and I shall have another judgment that will stipulate the meaning of (1). I could say, for instance that

(2) The man of the 18th Brumaire lost at Waterloo

or that

(3) The husband of Josephine lost at Waterloo

or that

(4) Napoleon was beaten at Waterloo

or that

(5) Napoleon lost his final battle in Waterloo (in Belgium),

and so forth. In (2) and (3) the reference is put on the subject, in (4) on the action, and in (5) on the place, because Waterloo is in Belgium and it is where Napoleon was once and for all defeated.

This analysis of (1) is really a standard one made on Fregean grounds. But we would like to know why all those propositions are equivalent, why they all have the same meaning. They obviously have the same reference, compositionally as well as globally.

The whole question is to discern *how* we know they have the same reference, how we get access to the factual identity of the terms involved in all those judgments. Once we have that knowledge, then we can affirm the substitutability of (1), (2), (3), (4), and (5), among other possibilities; but we cannot start by assuming their identical reference, because to do so begs the very question of substitutability. It is the concept of substitution that we want to explain here, so we must certainly not assume the identity *a priori* by saying that identical reference implies meaning as identity. In order to see *why* it is so, we must suppose that we know neither the reference nor the meaning of (1) and see how we get (2), (3), (4), or (5). If we accept not to beg the question of meaning and reference, we must actually raise it and not start as if the issue was already settled, as if all the answers were already, and always, at our disposal.

Let us now suppose that we do not understand (1). What would we ask to get its meaning? We could ask, for instance: *What,* or *who,* is that man (Napoleon)? If we know who he is, but not what he did, we could ask: What did Napoleon do at Waterloo? If we know all that, and if we do not understand (1), the only remaining possibility is that we do not understand what Waterloo is. Hence a last question: *What,* or *where,* is Waterloo? Or: What did happen at Waterloo? To the first group of questions, we have (2) and (3) as possible answers; to the second problem corresponds (4), and to the last one, (5). Meaning is an answer. It relates to the question it solves, by stipulating how it does it. To various questions correspond various answers. What matters now is to provide an analysis of the question-answer relationship which underlies meaning.

To each sentence, (1), (2), (3), (4), and (5), we can easily associate an interrogative clause without modifying either the truth-value or the signification of the propositions. Each interrogative clause takes up the questions that bear on the components of (1) and presents them as solved instead of merely answering them, but it amounts to the same thing, since the propositional content is preserved by transformation.

We could, therefore, say the following:

(2′) The man *who* made the 18th Brumaire lost at Waterloo.
(3′) The man *who* married Josephine lost at Waterloo.
(4′) Waterloo is a battle *which* Napoleon lost.
(5′) Waterloo is the Belgian town *where* Napoleon's final defeat took place.

Other versions, of course, could be given, but it would not alter the line of the argument. In order to specify the reference of the terms of proposition (1), we resort to interrogatives (and interrogative clauses) that express the questions raised by the interlocutor who does not understand some term in (1) and, as a result, (1) itself.

Let us now go one step further in the analysis. Each interrogative clause can be replaced by a term in itself, and the interrogative then disappears. The terms of judgments are the results of some solving-process; they correspond to the deleted interrogatives; they answer the question that might come up if some misunderstanding were to arise. Those terms are referential in virtue of the fact that no question is referred to but rather some other reality, that reality being precisely *what* is said through them, *what* they say and not their own "what-ness." Referentiality here is turned outward. The fact is that interrogative clauses are introduced in order to present the questions which could (or do) arise as solved. If we say, for instance, "The man who died in a car accident . . . ," we assume that he actually died in a car accident. This fact is out of the question. Similarly, when interrogatives are deleted and adjectives, for instance, are introduced in correspondence, the same effect of out-of-questionableness arises. "This stupid man did this" obviously assumes that the man is stupid; this is not the topic, the question, debated by this sentence. These effects just described have a strong rhetorical impact. They present as solved what could be debatable: If the man who died in a car accident is thought to have died sometime later, and if some people think he had been beaten by the police, we can easily imagine the rhetorical effect of such a phrase in court. If we want to speak of someone who did this or that, and at the same time devalue him without having to justify our claim, the second example above is also well suited. In both cases, the answer is offered as solving a question without really raising it thematically. The use of interrogative clauses or their deletion does the job quite well for the reasons we now can see: to speak is to answer, and the meaning of what we say is given by some underlying, or explicit, question-answer relationship. We could thus have the following substitutions for the examples (2) to (5) chosen previously:

(2″) The man of the 18th Brumaire lost at Waterloo.
(3″) Josephine's husband lost at Waterloo.
(4″) Napoleon was defeated at Waterloo.
(5″) Napoleon's final defeat was Waterloo.

If the locutor suppresses the interrogatives, it is because he thinks that nothing problematic remains to be taken up and expressed as solved by what he says. The deletion of interrogative clauses means that he supposes a great understanding, due, for instance, to background knowledge, on the part of his addressee. And the less the latter understands, or is supposed to understand, the more explicit the reference of the various terms should be made by additional embedded relative clauses. Those relatives stipulate the object of the questions that the interlocutor has in mind. When the interrogatives are deleted, it is because the questions which are treated by the locutor are considered (rightly or wrongly) as solved. The terms in question are deemed to be completely specified. This means that what they refer to does not raise any further question in the mind of the speaker. The world they describe, so to speak, is known as much as is necessary, and it does not have to be investigated further for the expressions at work to convey their full content and specification. The terms which appear in a proposition may, therefore, be considered as answers to the interrogatives. As they answer them, those interrogatives are rendered superfluous, hence they are deleted. The questions which could arise remain present in some manner, albeit tacitly, since such a term in the proposition is the marker of a solution. The absence of these interrogatives merely signifies that they are not problematic, that what they indicate is clear or assumed to be clear. *What* is affirmed is *known* and deemed to be known. No further question arises as to *what* is said, and therefore no interrogative appears to determine what is in question and to show that the proposition solves it by saying what it says. Interrogatives and interrogative clauses need not be mentioned when the sentence is semantically unproblematic. If, for instance, one did not know *who* Napoleon was, *what* the battle *in question* was, and what losing meant, questions would explicitly arise and proposition (1) would be reformulated accordingly, with the interrogative clauses specifying the reference of the problematic terms. The interrogative clauses can always be suppressed or avoided, even if they underlie the assertions proffered. It is a matter of comprehension, or rather, of the degree in comprehension. "Napoleon, *who* was Josephine's husband, lost at Waterloo" is more informative about Napoleon than, say, (1) taken alone.

4. JUDGMENTS AS ANSWERS

What has always been called a judgment or a proposition is nothing but an answer. Answers do not present themselves as such. What gives rise to the answer is some problem, some question to be treated, which disappears once solved. This is why the problematic elements are suppressed and absent in the answer. The latter in turn does not refer anymore to the question(s) which has (or have) disappeared through the answering process. This explains why the answer does not appear as an *answer,* but as a mere statement, whose origin is irrelevant to its "value," i.e., to what it asserts, its truth. As a result, the answer, instead of expressing itself as an answer referring to some previous question(s), refers to *what* it solves. The solution it offers is given by the terms it contains. Those terms are themselves the results of an answering process which includes the referents of the deleted interrogatives. Answerhood, in this respect, is referential, and at the same time ascribes a meaning to the answer. Meaning is no reference *per se,* but they are connected because meaning is the expression of answerhood in language, and that answerhood, here, exhibits a referential structure since it bears on the terms of some single answers. When the question of meaning bears on several statements considered as a whole (i.e., as a textual unit), or does not bear on the literal structure of a given statement, the equation of referentiality as meaningfulness ceases to be valid. The answerhood of a text is something else. It cannot be found in the same way, but meaning remains given by the problematic dealt with in and by the text as a whole. We do not deny that such a problematic is, in some manner, rooted in what the text *literally* asserts. In fact, it is even *implied* in such a literality. That is why understanding always amounts to the *derivation* of an implied "message." Implication and derivation are always associated in reading and understanding.

Let us now go back to literal meaning to further explain why and how propositions should be conceived as answers, so that we may (a) better understand how language works, and (b) see that there is no semantic gap between propositional units and textual ones.

First, to the question "Who lost at Waterloo?" we can always reply "Napoleon," instead of "Napoleon lost at Waterloo." The full answer is not necessary because, in some way, the respondent assumes the following expression to be true: "Napoleon is the answer." But this answerhood is not mentioned, though it could be. The single word *Napoleon* is what saturates the question, and this is why it is sufficient to mention it. A full statement would also saturate the question, since it is an answer which is expected, and an answer is, from the point of view of the surface structure, a statement.

Second, we observe that, if we ask what happened at Waterloo, we can indifferently answer that Napoleon lost the battle or that it was Napoleon's final defeat; any other statement from (2″) to (5″) would be a correct answer. Similarly we could easily ascribe different questions to one given answer: "What did Napoleon do at Waterloo?" and "Who was Napoleon?" could be answered by saying that "He is the man *who* lost at Waterloo," for instance. This interrogative "*who*" functions as an answering-marker for the question raised. The important point here is that several questions can be *derived* from a given answer, as if, actually or not, they had been raised (by the locutor) to be answered. The answer can then mean several things, and each meaningful reading can be derived as an implied problematological answer, i.e., a statement expressing the question solved.

Third, if we recognize the role of interrogatives in the underlying structure of statements, we can better understand the nature of judgment at large. Why is a judgment composed of a subject and a predicate? The main reason appears to be the need to establish, in language, what is out of the question, which is assumed or presupposed, and the answer to that very question. Both components of this difference should be represented, even when there is no interrogative or interrogative clause. If the question is "What happened at Waterloo?" and if we answer that Napoleon lost a battle there, we take up something which is in question and relate it to the event, the action and its agent. As to *being,* it is nothing other than the verb that expresses the problematological difference between question and answer, the differentiation *and* the dynamic of their linkage in language. We could also ask, for instance, "Who was Napoleon?" and answer "He was the man *who* lost at Waterloo," or, if we want to delete the interrogative, "Napoleon was the loser of the battle of

Waterloo." Napoleon's "being" is, in a sense, in question, and this is why
he appears as the subject of the answer. Here we assume that we know
the meaning of Waterloo's battle, or at least that we know enough of it to
characterize Napoleon.

Let us go one step further. We consider that a judgment, being an
answer referring in some way to a problem, is made of a problematic
element and an apocritic one. The apocritic element is that which itself
is not the subject of the question but enables the locutor to answer it
instead. "What did Napoleon do at Waterloo?" This question presupposes
that Napoleon did x at Waterloo, and the answer will tell us that he did
something *which* is called a defeat, i.e. (after interrogative deletion), that
he *lost* at Waterloo. "Who was the loser at Waterloo?" This is another
question: some x lost at Waterloo, and it is out of the question that
Waterloo was x's defeat. "Napoleon lost at Waterloo" is also the answer.

We could multiply examples of this kind, in which something is problematic and something is not, in order to explain why we find both
elements in what is offered as the answer. In other words, we could
define a judgment as an *x-structure,* in which the x could express predicates as well as subjects, being given that either the subject or the
predicate should be specified as nonproblematic if the other element
appears as problematic. Proper names and adjectives ("the man, *who*
did . . . ," for "the courageous man," for instance), as much as predicates,
are the outcome of interrogative deletion. Interrogative expansion,
through embedding, forms the basis of generative grammar, just as the x-
structure serves as the ultimate foundation for the logic of language,
even though its function is essentially propositionalist.

We now fully realize why and when meaning is referential. Meaning, as
Wittgenstein once said,[3] is the answer to the question of meaning. An
answer gives its meaning implicitly, but when explicitly asked its answerhood must be exhibited through language. The content, however,
i.e., *what* is said, remains identical, since the initial proposition was
already an answer, although not reflexively, not thematically so. Meaning
is the question-answer relationship inherent in any discourse, but only
revealed as such when some question is asked as to what might be in
question in what was said. This relationship will be referential when the
question of meaning bears upon some given proposition, i.e., on some
terms involved in the statement. The referential structure of the statement emerges as a by-product of the question-answer relationship. If one
denies any role to questioning, as propositionalism has always done,
meaning simply appears as referentiality. And this, of course, is only

partially true: it only applies to propositional terms and completely leaves aside the process through which meaning is produced, enacted upon receivers, or brought to the fore. Such a process is not incidental. Meaning is not referential when texts are considered, because the question of meaning there ceases to bear upon terms but bears instead on the whole, whose problematic must be discovered. Nonetheless, there is meaning involved in textual discourse, because it is an answer whose question is precisely the object of the question of meaning. Referentiality is therefore one aspect, one by-product, of what meaning is all about, and meaning cannot as a consequence be reduced to mere reference and everything else eliminated. What is constant, however, is that meaning is answerhood. When it does not have to be specified, but is merely exhibited unreflexively, on what is in question appears, thought not as being what is *in question*. This referential structure has been known in other times as the structure of consciousness, which is intentional. Consciousness *is,* insofar as it relates to something else. This will turn out later to be the constitutive feature of the *sign* in semiotics and structuralism. Consciousness is transcendental in the sense that it is directed toward the object and at the same time toward itself in a potential way. The point made here is that consciousness, as well as the sign, are in reality problematological structures though unperceived so far. They enable us to *seek* and *find* (ourselves) in a world, and this recalls Kant's famous query: *"Was heißt sich im Denken orientieren?"*

The signs, or consciousness, reveal themselves as historical stages of the answerhood of reason. They are stages within the propositionalist view of rationality, as opposed to the problematological one. Consciousness and "signifiers" relate to *what* they denote by letting what-ness appear, although, at a second level of inquiry, consciousness could be directed toward itself to answer the question of meaning, as much as signs could become their own object, without causing any change in meaning. In the questioning process, *what* is in question emerges as out-of-the-question. Questioning itself is repressed in favor of its reference through an answer which does not affirm itself as an answer, although it could, if necessary, in order to allow for understanding. Consciousness, as much as language, through signs, possesses this feature, which enables us to know the world and to find what we look for. For propositionalism, language has a structure of its own, independent of consciousness, and this structure implies a different way of access to true propositions. What-ness without questioning should now be replaced by what-ness as relating to problems.

5. FROM SENTENTIAL SEMANTICS TO HERMENEUTICS

A lot has been said about hermeneutics since Dilthey and Schleier-macher. The nineteenth century ends with a crisis which shall be known as the "crisis of the subject." This means nothing else but the death of the subject, or transcendental ego. The ego ceases to be considered as a starting point or a foundation; instead of being the source of any possible determination, it was itself determined. Consciousness is conditioned by unconscious motives (Freud), by historical interest, of which it is hardly aware for the most part (Marx), when it is not simply a fiction to curb our will to affirm ourselves as individuals (Nietzsche).[4] Subjects ceased then to be considered "pure" and, as Foucault has shown, the death of the pure subject coincided with the birth of the *Geisteswissenschaften.*[5] Human subjectivity, by losing its ontological aloofness, became an object like any other, and consequently could be studied like any object, with the reservation, nonetheless, that those "human sciences" were much less deterministic than the natural sciences or mathematics.

Understanding, as opposed to explanation, is the concept that captures the alternatives of human behavior. There is no necessity to act in one way rather than in another, even though there are grounds, unconscious or not, which explain behavior, i.e., enable us to understand why somebody has acted the way he has rather than otherwise. Understanding, being based on the notion of alternative, is a problematological concept, even though it has been epistemologized under the influence of propositionalism, in contradistinction to the necessity of deterministic discourse, the external model of the propositional *logos,* the ultimate value of reference being apodicticity.

In reality, understanding is not a weak, i.e., nondeterministic, form of knowledge or reasoning; it is a form of questioning, as is mathematics. Understanding is interpretative: it raises a question on or about another question, for which only the answer is at our disposal. Hence the plurality of hermeneutic answers concerning the interpretation of a given solution. Interpretation can be as elaborate as it wishes, but it is bound to remain problematic to some degree. To see how hermeneutics works, let us consider the example of the interpretation of the history of philosophy, in which controversial readings seem more widespread than elsewhere.

Let us envisage one fairly well-known instance of philosophical interpretation. Why does Plato put forth his paradox in the *Meno,* which comes down to the affirmation that to acquire knowledge is impossible? "A man cannot inquire about what he knows or about what he does not know. For he cannot inquire about what he knows, because he knows it, and in this case, he has no need of inquiry; nor again can he inquire about what he does not know, since he does not know about what he is to inquire" (*Meno,* 80e). What will be Plato's way out of this double bind? We could say that there is such a paradox because knowledge is acquired through reminiscence. This explains why it is either impossible to look for truth, or useful when we should be in a position to do so. We have forgotten what we do not know, though at the same time we know it is a sense, i.e., have this knowledge in our minds. It is therefore possible to know, i.e., to recall, and useful, since we have forgotten.

We can contest this solution because, in fact, it displaces and reproduces the problem. If I know what I have to remember, I already know it, and it is useless to remember what is present in my consciousness. And if I do not know what I should recall, how can I possibly know what to remember and how shall I remember what I do not know that I have to remember?—the same dilemma as in Meno's paradox.

What has now happened to Plato's solution? In a sense we could say that it has been "refuted" as an argument, from the point of view of its validity. But we could also say that we face the same problem as in the *Meno;* the problem of the acquisition of knowledge, a problem which only arises because, Plato could reply, we fail to see that knowledge is only remembrance, and that it is triggered under the pressure of external factors.

The important point here is not to defend or to attack Plato's solution; it is to see what we do when we interpret it, let alone reject it. If we accept the argument, we accept the solution to the problem that it raises. If we do not, we reject the *solution,* i.e., a relationship with a question.Reminiscence, being inadequate as a solution, leaves the problem of knowledge intact. The answer is not refuted as a piece of false discourse, it is simply refused as answer. Then knowledge, appearing again as a problem, is seen differently.

Alternatively, with respect to the answer that Plato offers, the answer remains valid, so to speak; it is not deemed false but reinterpreted as problematic instead, as *meaning* something else. To reject a statement as an answer does not imply that we reject the statement altogether, but only in relationship with the question that it *means* to solve. As a result, the problem is maintained through the solution, which is seen as one of its expressions, rather than as what makes it disappear once and for all. On the other hand, we can accept the solution as definitive or consider the problem as being "uninteresting." The basic presupposition is that the doctrine under examination raises some question. This, in turn, implies that the past will provide some answer, directly or indirectly; directly if in the past the question of the present has been explicitly raised, e.g., the problem of knowledge in Plato; indirectly if we can *derive* the solution of the past. Something can be in question in what is said, "objectively," if we wish to put it that way, even though the question has not been thematically expressed as such beforehand. *Derived* questions require that the interpreter infer them. That is why hermeneutics is *inference*, but problematological inference, a link between questions and answers. Referentiality only allows for literal answers; one can derive what is in question from what is said, whereas figurative reading must be elaborated, i.e., inferred via *other* answers. Derived questions are those questions that the present invites us to search for in the solutions of the past. Since they can be found in the past, we can conclude that those questions were already there, and our present questions are therefore the product of some historical evolution. This explains why hermeneutical questions are seldom arbitrary when addressed to the past, where they can be in some way derived, even though not explicitly questioned at that time. The autonomization of a given problem in some given present is history itself. And the reading of history is hermeneutical, in the sense that we try to discover the problems beneath or behind the solutions of other related problems, the latter being the problems "of the time."

The reading of meaning is, then, an inferential process based on the articulation of what is problematic and what is not. It can be inferred directly, i.e., literally, through the use of interrogatives and relative clauses, and the various possible questions at stake will be brought to light. Or it can be inferred indirectly, figuratively, as a derived problem which is not the problem directly derivable from what is said. The reading of meaning will then be more inferential, less referential, and based on external factors, such as the context or other texts, or history, for instance. The more figurative a reading, the more problematic it is bound to be. The isolated judgment, i.e., referentiality, ceases to be the key, and, as such, from the hermeneutic point of view, it is problematic as to what is in question in what it propounds. This requires a solution from the receiver, from the reader, who is increasingly questioned when figurativity is all the more expressed. If referentiality is the measure of our everyday real world, we can then assert that fictionality also increases with figurativity and derivation. The answer is no longer the text itself, not the judgment alone; as a result, problematicity is all the more increasing, with its natural consequence: the increased multiplicity of answers expressing meaning, up to the point where the only remaining possible answer is problematicity itself. Fiction, then, becomes closed to any (literal) interpretation but the avowal of this impossibility. Contemporary literature, and its counterpart, deconstructionism, illustrate my point here. But basically, any interpretation deals with problematicity, whether it is more or less affirmed. The example we have borrowed from the history of philosophy shows that we relate to answers in function of problems which render those very answers more or less problematic, i.e., acceptable or not, in need of other answers because the questions are seen otherwise, i.e., contemporarily, each time.

Let us now expound the general view of language upon which our analyses rest.

6. THE QUESTION-VIEW OF LANGUAGE

Linguistic activity at large, and not only literature, is ruled by the laws of questioning. We speak and write with a question in mind, a problem to solve that we communicate when we expect the solution from someone else, or about which we talk by sharing its solution with our interlocutor. Propositions are then answers, as Collingwood suggested long ago in his *Autobiography,* although without developing fully the consequences of such a view. The basic distinction upon which it rests is the *problematological difference,* which enables language-users to recognize and differentiate questions and answers, and thereby to realize what is expected of them in a given context. Either we face a question or we deal with an answer, and the difference has always to be marked off in some way. One of the most elementary ways of marking this difference is, of course, by recourse to a certain form, such as the interrogative one; but one might also employ the imperative, which expresses problems, or the declarative, which asserts solutions. Form is all the more necessary to mark the problematological difference in instances where the context does not enable the addressee to determine it with the available tacit knowledge of the locutor's problems *and* answers on given problems. The context plays the role of a problematological differentiator, so to speak. When it provides enough information on what is problematic and what is out-of-the-question in a definite situation, linguistic forms can be used for other purposes than to mark the problematological difference for the addressee.

The problematological difference is at work at all levels of language. From its semantics to its rhetoric, from the hermeneutical relationship to the dialogical, the unity and functioning of language rests upon this difference.

Let us first consider the assertoric dimension, with which questioning seems to have nothing whatsoever to do. An assertion is a proposition whose meaning is given by its truth-conditions, whose aim is to describe something of reality. There is, therefore, no question at stake in such a linguistic form. This is, of course, the *credo* of propositionalism, as we have inherited it from the Greeks. The theory of judgment it expresses is based on the idea of semantic autonomy. Propositionalism claims that propositions can be studied in and of themselves, independently of any context of utterance, that they can be isolated for the purpose of study, as they are in textbooks of logic and linguistics, because they would occur as such. This Platonism can still be found in contemporary thought. It has been codified by Frege and his followers, Bertrand Russell, and, to a lesser extent, Wittgenstein. Language, according to such thinkers, is made up of propositions and is always reducible to them, however complex it may appear.

This view has not withstood careful examination. Many sentences are not propositions, nor are they reducible to a literalization of their content, which would be presupposed as propositional. Besides, nobody ever utters isolated sentences independent of any context or of other sentences. They do not exist in and by themselves. They are always related in some way or other, and what they mean is not always expressible by another proposition stating their truth-conditions. If the meaning of a statement is another statement, should we say that the meaning of *Don Quixote,* for instance, is its rewriting? This would lead to the paradox of *Don Xerox,* which ensues from the propositionalization of meaning in the sphere of textuality and fiction. Meaning, rather, is given by what is in question in that which is said. We remember Sartre's example at the beginning of *Being and Nothingness,* where someone enters a café and says "Peter is not here!" Such a statement cannot be understood without reference to the locutor's problem, which is to find Peter, to see whether he is in the café or not. The proposition is nothing but an answer to that question and cannot be understood independently of it. The utterance is not the description of some mysterious nothingness inscribed in the fullness of Being, but more simply, perhaps, one of the two possible answers to the question that the speaker has in mind when he goes into that café.

A proposition such as "The cat is on the mat" gives it meaning by the question it deals with, even if what is in question is not literally stated as such. The answerhood of propositions is something which is assumed in this case. The meaning is not given in the sense that the statement would affirm "This is what I answer," but it is nonetheless there, underlying all possible intelligibility. Let us note that the meaning of some term or other could become problematic, and then the question is some being which..." or "The mat is something *that*..." Each time, we would have an interrogative, taking up the question in the answer itself and expressing it as being solved. The proposition is an answer which could always reveal itself as such if necessary. The answer then affirms the meaning which presents itself first as its implicit content. It expresses what is in question and explicitly differentiates itself from it. If the meaning here is referential, it is because the interrogatives state *what* the terms refer to. The conflation of reference and meaning is an error stemming from the denial of the role of questioning. Where we have nonreferential language, such as fiction, we still have meaning as answerhood, that is, as a question-answer relationship, but the questions raised are not based upon *terms* and their explication.

When you say that Napoleon lost at Waterloo, there is the *question* of Napoleon, of *what* he did and *where*. If I know the answers to these questions, I shall have understood you; and if you do not specify the questions you are dealing with, it is because you deem them answered by what you say, and sufficiently so. The questions raised are raised as solved, through their solution. You think, therefore, that I shall understand your statement right away. But let us suppose that somebody comes to you on the street and suddenly tells you "Napoleon lost at Waterloo." You really do not know what he means, even if you understand each term. The reason is that you do not know *why* this person says this to you, the problem he has in mind *when* he says it, the question *which* underlies its utterance. What is in question is some query other than the one literally dealt with. Figurativity is a problematological notion, but we only know it in its propositional version, in terms of the opposition between the literal and the figurative. We generally acknowledge only a correlative concern to establish a priority between them, and see the other as a derivative, reflexive, and secondary use of the first[6]—Frege *versus* Nietzsche and Derrida. Why is the duality of the literal and the figurative propositional? The answer lies in the fact that these concepts do not refer in any way to the problematological nature of the duality, to the fact that they are related like question and answer. The example given above illustrates this clearly. The utterance "Napoleon lost at Waterloo" raises the question of what it means, i.e., of what is in question, of the problem it answers. Such a problem is bound to arise because the sentence does not answer any question in the context evoked in the example, which is a context of absence of common presuppositions with regard to the questions, and therefore to the solutions, shared.

The interlocutor is then questioned with regard to the question of the locutor; his answer will provide the missing question, and it will stipulate the answerhood of the answer by another statement. This is what we usually mean by a *why-question* (or a *why-answer*): it relates two statements in such a way that the answer to the first question enables us to arrive at the answer to the second; this answer is suggested by the question *implied* in the first answer. Implication, impliedness, inference, even implicature, all these notions are closely linked. This, I think, renders full justice to the traditional dichotomy in rhetoric between the *rhetoric of conflicts* (Aristotle, Perelman) and the *rhetoric of figures* (Barthes, Gérard Genette, et al.). In both cases we have a question, and we have to infer the answer, whether or not there is a conflict of answers or a sheer evocation of this answer. A literary critic, a reader, is as much a reasoner as the judge in the court, because he is a questioner in both cases, a questioner of the question raised, of the adequacy of the answer offered. The duality of meaning is inscribed within the very nature of language, as being its capacity to evoke, to raise, to suggest a question by the answers it provides to nonexplicitly specified questions previously expressed. If someone says to me "It's one o'clock," since I did not ask the question it must answer another question which arises in the context, for instance whether it is time to have lunch. As a result, it is an answer whose question is asked of me. My answer will tell what the *locutor's* answer was actually answering. The duality of meaning induces the reader to have an active role, whereas the literal answer tells him all that can be expected *a priori.*

The double reading of answers is rooted in their very answerhood. They raise a question not necessarily the same as the one they solve, because the question is not fully specified or even known on the basis of the context. Since the object of the question is not to assert itself as a question but to assert the solution, a figurative reading is always possible, as is a literal one implying the figurative.

The duality of meaning is therefore a rupture in the usual course of expectations: a literal reading stops the questioning process, while the other activates it. In other words, the rhetoric of language stems from the fact that a question arises, on which the reader (the listener, addressee, etc.) is asked to infer the answer, i.e., to conclude something which is not literally said. Let us imagine that I ask a girl to have a walk with me. She replies "The weather is nice, but it's too cold for me." This answer obviously takes up the two sides of the alternative. "The weather is nice" suggests that she accepts, whereas "it's too cold for me" rather indicates the opposite. Has she then really offered an answer? Literally, she has merely repeated the problem. Nevertheless, everybody will have understood that her reply *meant* a negative answer to the invitation. If she simply wanted to say yes, she would have said it, without mentioning any negative argument. If she adds a negative argument to the positive one, it is in order to counterbalance whatever positive can be said about my invitation. If she does so, it is because she questions the positive argument, and the negative argument is therefore seen as stronger and leads me to infer the negative as being *the* conclusion to the "debate." This is not literally affirmed, but it is done figuratively.

Figurativity is a process based upon the questioning of the reader. The more a text is figurative, rhetorical in the sense just defined, the more it asks the reader to *seek* what is meant. The interrogative nature of language implies the constant possibility of rhetoricity, which can be intentionally and systematically organized by the "implicitation" of the questions at stake in the text, which in turn are to be found and questioned by the addressee since they *are* the problem.

7. THE BASIC LAW OF FICTION

We have seen why rhetoric is an inherent dimension of any linguistic activity and how it functions in principle. It is rooted in the fact that linguistic usage is always a reply to some problem, and that raising a problem may be the object of the answer itself.

Literary rhetoric is not different in this respect. The law of complementarity between form and context upholds that when the context is rich in information on the problematic, form can be diverted from the necessity to express the problematological difference. Literature cannot rely on any shared and precise context, wherein both the author and the reader would find a basis of evidence enabling them to differentiate the problematic and the apocritic beforehand. We can speak of common values, or even of a wide repertoire defining a common referential framework for discourse,[7] but we must not forget that this repertoire is indefinite. To whom in particular is the text addressed? What is supposed to be known by the addressee? Is not fiction rather an appeal to what is not factual? All these questions point to the fact that the context of reading has to be re-created or evoked in the text itself in order for the reader to select the relevant features of a possible common context. This I have called auto-contextualization; it is something that the text itself has to produce. This is why many reality-oriented texts speak about houses, trees, human beings doing this or that—all things we see in everyday life, but ones that must be represented and described first. As Wolfgang Iser puts it, "if the literary communication is to be successful it must bring with it all the components necessary for the construction of the situation since this has no existence outside the literary work."[8] But we remember that context has the specific role of problematological differentiation. Form, therefore, has to do it all in the fictional context. The consequences of the *law of complementarity* in language, when applied to fictional language, is what I have called the *law of inverse problematicity.*

What does it affirm? It affirms that the more explicit the problem is in the text, the more literal the demarcation between the problem and the solution. One passes from the problem to the solution quite progressively; fiction is all the more referential since it reproduces ordinary time and reality in their evolutive character. Fiction emphasizes the plot and its resolution by the explicitness of the problematic, of the intrigue at stake. The mimetic, referential structure of fiction is greater because the problem is literally represented, as well as its solution. The reader is more passive, and if he gets captured by the plot he will be led by the resolution as expounded and intended by the author.

Conversely, the less a problem is explicit, the more enigmatic the form will be rendered—through style, mode of expression, or textual arrangement, for example. This must be so according to the absolute requirement posed by the problematological difference. The auto-contextualizing process of fiction implies that this difference must be present, in one way or another, in the text itself as the structure of its very textuality.

Several consequences ensue from this law of inverse problematicity, or law of symbolic weakening.

First, the less explicit the problem, the more figurative the text, so as to express the problematicity not found in the text itself, but through the text. Symbolism, metaphoricity, and the duality of reading will be strengthened.

Second, the role of the reader will be all the more active, and constitutive, since the text is perceived as a question, instead of delivering itself as the answer which the reader had to assimilate. An extreme situation in this respect can be found in Calvino's *If on a Winter's Night a Traveller,* where the reader steps into the story and thereby makes it, by being the real object of the fiction itself. In fact, the reader is the main character of the novel. "Watch out: it is surely a method of involving you gradually, capturing you in the story before you realize it; a trap."[9]

The novel begins with a scene which takes place at the station, somewhere, anywhere, the place at which one arrives and leaves, the Place *par excellence,* where we all are, at any time, because *there* is *time.* "For a couple of pages now you have been reading on, and this would be the time to tell you clearly whether this station where I have got off is a station of the past or a station of today; instead the sentences continue to move in vagueness, grayness, in a kind of no man's land experience reduced to the lowest common denominator."[10] The reader is like this traveler lost in this station: it could be anybody and anywhere. The reader in the novel is, in fact, the novel as a problem for the reader, a problem which renders the story a real enigma as to its beginning, its process, the alternatives left open or suggested. "Perhaps this is why the author piles supposition on supposition in long paragraphs without dialogue, a thick, opaque layer of lead where I may pass unnoticed, disappear."[11] Who am "I"? "I am an anonymous presence against an even more anonymous background ... this is the only thing you know about me, but this alone is reason enough for you to invest a part of yourself in the stranger 'I.' "[12] The reader is this stranger, he is part of the story, he makes it. The following chapter will even describe the reaction of the reader when he finishes the first chapter.

Third, the plurality of equally plausible interpretations, based on the subjectivity of reading as much as on the constraints of the interpreted text, will increase with the figurativity, i.e., enigmaticity, of literature. What fiction asks is less and less an interpretation which would be an answer; this increased problematicity is itself the answer. I have called this a problematological answer, because the text, as answer, bears upon itself as a question—it means to express a problem without any answer other than the expression of the problem itself. This metafictional, self-referential feature is a characteristic of extreme figurativity. A good example of this can be found in Kafka's famous text *Die Prüfung* (*The Text*), which has been analyzed above.

Fourth, and finally, the more figurative a text is, the greater its problematicity. A gap between the fiction and the reader arises which is usually associated with dereferentialization, or *"entpragmatisierung."* When the progression of the textual arrangement is a linear resolution based on literal elements as found in the real world, there is a strong commonality between the text and the reader, a commonality which falls apart when the figurative aspects increase—i.e., when the reader is put into question and compelled to realize that there is no common ground anymore, due to the questioning of referentiality as the key to meaning. Quite obviously, the First World War has created the historical conditions for such a break with the world as it was. Discontinuity arose with the loss of stability of the world, calling into question the common ground and the basic ethical values of Europe. Hence Joyce, Hermann Hesse, and Musil, for instance. Radical problematicity, viewed as the realization of nihilism and its antihumanism, became the key phrase. The optimism of the Kantian subject was broken, and the unitary point of view in fiction—with its correlates, the beginning and the end, the linearity of the resolution process of the plot and of the intrigue— gradually vanished, as in the *nouveau roman*.

Let us now conclude. The possible variation of the figurative character of texts is ruled by the requirement of the problematological difference. In all the above examples, the minimal figurative meaning is the implicit question-answer relationship embedded in the text. When this relationship becomes its own object, in fiction, figurativity has reached an extreme. But even when it is literally figured out, it nonetheless underlies any reading, as it is its ultimate condition of possibility.

6

The Rationality of Knowledge

1. THE POSITIVIST CONCEPTION

Т his chapter presents a view of science, which I have had the opportunity to expound in greater detail in French,[1] that serves as an alternative to neopositivism and to the conception which succeeded it (grounded primarily in the history of science).

Neopositivism, by analyzing scientific judgments considered in themselves, as if they belonged to an autonomous world of free-floating results, hoped to discover the secret of what made them scientific. It obviously failed:[2] a sentence which purports to be scientific is not, *in itself,* more scientific than one that does not, and no viable criterion of scientific empiricalness has been discovered. This was much to the disappointment of the positivists, who, criterion after criterion, had to put up with the impossibility of digging up the ultimate foundation of rationality from the mere results of linguistic activity, as if the latter could be scientific by itself. Science, reduced to those results, ended up on the same level as the other types of discourse from which the positivists strove to demarcate it. Refutability, on the other hand, is not sufficient to distinguish scientific propositions from those that are not. A valid scientific theory cannot be said to have been refuted as long as it is deemed valid, no more than can a nonscientific theory which is assumed to be valid, though incorrectly in the light of future developments. Perhaps the former is refutable whereas the latter is not, but, in this case, the property of falsifiability cannot be one of language. Refutability is not an attribute that a sentence (or a set of sentences) considered as a piece of language[3] possesses or does not possess in virtue of its logical or grammatical form alone.

Positivism, nonetheless, thought it could discover the secret of scientificalness by analyzing the sole language used in science, as if the sentences put forward contained their scientific features in their very structure. By doing so, it inevitably took up existing science and strenuously sought for a discursivity *sui generis.* Scientific statements, by being scientific, ought to reveal scientificalness. Is not science the autonomous discourse *par excellence,* unlike natural languages, which require a context of utterance in order to be intelligible? Scientific propositions are interrelated, insofar as each is either the consequence or the ground of the other (or both). Justification makes science closed upon itself: even primary propositions are justified in that closed space by being fruitful within it.

Positivism, proceeding in this way, limited itself to the study of established knowledge as it has sedimented in scientific theories. The process through which such a knowledge is attained was totally overlooked. The results seemed to only stem from themselves. Their elaboration, therefore, fell outside of science, in which what counts as scientific belongs to the sphere of what has been successfully submitted to justification, i.e., to the appropriate logico-experimental procedures. Discovery, being the process through which an original solution is brought to a problem, is the concern of psychology, and not of philosophy, when it is not simply conflated with the justification process.

Nonetheless, it would be misleading to focus only on the answers research has led to and to make them the whole of science, as if the questions which rendered them possible were unessential in the answering process. The epistemologist would be in the same situation as a medical doctor who set himself the task of studying life only by carrying out autopsies. The reduction of science, of the whole research process, which comprehends both the questions and the answers, to its finished products arranged quite neatly in a perfectly logical order where all the problematic aspects have been removed would be like equating the size of an iceberg to its emerged part. Positivists sometimes admit that science undergoes progress, but they conceive this extension of knowledge in terms of results only, and they offer us, as a result, a cumulative view of knowledge, in which judgments are added to other judgments, without any loss or replacement, as if those ceased to be scientific once they were superseded. In the positivist account, there is no room left for errors and unsuccessful attempts, even though the statements resulting from them were produced according to the standards of logico-experimental procedures characteristic of scientific investigation.

Judging, instead of answering, is the synthetic part of science, its basic unit, according to positivism. There is, of course, no linguistic or grammatical distinction between an answer and a statement. The latter is merely a static concept, and as such it does not indicate that it could result from a global activity exceeding its own production and which should be called science. The notion of answer refers back to questioning (or problem solving) to the extent that it is necessarily inserted within a dialectical process in which there are questions because there are answers. Questions and answers constitute different entities, but they also refer to different attitudes, since they both pertain to the scientific *process*. Moreover, being complementary to one another, they overlap. If questions can, and should, be analyzed independently of their corresponding answers in order to discover whether they obey a logic of their own, they should be brought into relationship with their answers in a structural view.

In order to shed light on the specificity of the conception I wish to advocate here, I shall hark back to the theory of science which speaks of statements rather than answers.

Such an attitude reflects the decision to focus on the established body of knowledge and to study it thoroughly. But this standpoint leads to a vision of science which only takes language into account. That is why positivists have studied so much the syntax and the logic of scientific language, and so little the dynamics of science, which they amalgamated with a succession of valid statements. Logicisim was the outcome.

Statements present what is the case, they refer to states of affairs, they have a constatative value, and they are deprived of the performative and contextual elements which are inherent in any linguistic activity. They do not seem to address themselves to anybody, and thereby they appear to be final and out-of-the-question, as if they belonged to the past and had nothing to do with science in the making. Their very presence might even reveal that some questions, which they had answered, should never be raised afresh. Further research is then totally alien to them. They are results, and only results count in science. Positivism dooms to failure all attempts to account for scientific growth, insofar as it rejects what the findings result from, as if this were not already science. Results seem to spring forth spontaneously, and what is prior to this level is either a mere psychological process or, since science is not irrational, a modality of justification, in which, however, the scientist deals with what must have been found before.

2. SCIENCE AS A TWO-LEVEL PROCESS

The reality of the scientific process is totally different from the positivist's description of it. The scientist who endeavors to account for each of his answers must already have found them. To have done so, he had to investigate those questions which ultimately correspond to them. Science is a questioning process, and if its language is to be described it must be done in terms of answers and not statements. This evidently lays the basis for a radically new conception of language, as it was programmatically outlined by Collingwood more than fifty years ago. The questions which are raised by the scientist are obviously not interrogative sentences. Such sentences are used by a questioner to elicit an answer or, if the latter is not verbal (e.g., "*Would you please shut the door?*"), a solution from another person. The scientist, if he is to advance *global* knowledge, must find the answer by himself. Nobody else already has it, and therefore questions do not need to be formulated: they are treated as problems or puzzles. Ordinary language confirms this; for example, we say "*to treat a problem*" or that we are going to consider "*what is in question*" in a discourse to indicate that we are going to examine what a discourse is about, which problem is raised by it.

Questioning and looking for an answer to one or several problems cannot necessarily be equated with science. There are other questioning processes—ours, for example, whose object is science and which is philosophical. What is then the specificity of science? In reality, our interest in science derives from the fact that it implements a rationality defined as questioning. What is this rationality which characterizes the transition from questions to answers? How does questioning work in science? These are our questions, once we have realized that science should be conceived as a questioning-process rather than as consisting in a network of already-justified, and thereby inert, statements. Paradoxical as it may seem, the distinction between science and other questioning processes is secondary. The paradox, however, is only one in appearance. The features of a science ultimately are to be found in its particular methodology. One justification procedure rather than another is chosen not only because of the object under study but also because of the traditional requirements adopted by the scientific community to whom the results are addressed. The results in physics are no longer defined (and justified) along the same lines as they were in the time of Aristotle, nor even as they were by Newton. Similarly, the role as model that physico-mathematical science represented in the eyes of all scientists has gradually faded with the prodigious development of the social and historical sciences. We now recognize both their status as sciences and their right to adopt methodologies of their own. Even if the logico-experimental procedure, by which results are verified and justified, guarantees in each case that these results are indeed scientific, it nonetheless varies from science to science and from one period to another. Nowadays, the word *justification* covers a great variety of methodologies. The characteristic of science is lost in what we can call the context of justification, which varies in content from one science to another and which embraces both experimental verification and the exposition (i.e., the logical rearrangement) of the results. Whence the apparent paradox: science is best understood by not looking into its "specific difference" but rather by seeking to learn how it works. By limiting ourselves to the study of criteria of scientific justification, we would incur the risk and the reproach of favoring one type of science (e.g., physics) against all the others *or* of granting to the second stage of the scientific process an exaggerated importance, while the process as a whole would be disregarded and its first stage might even be negated as falling outside science. Positivism did all that. Our task is rather to investigate *how* science functions as a questioning process, independently of knowing what, here and then, is admitted as an answer (and this would imply the subsidiary questions *how* and *why*) and of knowing which questions are raised, here and then. The reduction of rationality to historical considerations, or to considerations drawn from the history of science, blurs the issue when it does not lead to mere falsity, even if it represents now a fashionable alternative to positivism. It leaves intact the problem of knowing how, at a given time, the scientist operates. The history of science provides empirical evidence for philosophers' theories, but it cannot serve as a substitute for them. When it does, it is as an unavowed theory of science which does not explicitly explain scientific investigation, because, as such, it could not. How can facts be selected, if not on the basis of theory? We can find in time a dimension of events, not their cause. I do not deny that what counts as an answer, and even as a problem, is historically conditioned. I only wish to claim that science is a questioning process in which questions and answers interact in a way that I would like to exhibit with a new and appropriate language. The specificity of science becomes a side issue for the epistemologist. It leads him to distinguish science from discourse devoid of scientific significance, and it is as futile as it is fruitless. Even if we could bring to light the necessary and sufficient conditions for what counts as scientific against what does not, we would not tell thereby how science *operates.* As to the deductive-nomological model, it fails to provide those conditions because, first, it is impossible to define a scientific law without falling into a vicious circle, and, second, because any argument can always be transformed into a deductive one by addition of ad hoc premises. What matters is not the logical texture and the methodological pecularity of the results, but rather the fact that this network is made up of answers and that they refer back to a level of questions. In this regard, science shares its rationality with other forms of knowledge from which it must not be cut off if, for example, one does not want the study of science to be deprived of rationality and cognitivity simply because it is not itself scientific. Science cannot be conceived of as the privileged locus of knowledge; otherwise, philosophy of science would be devoid of cognitive value. A question-view of science enables us to do this, for we are ourselves questioning science, which is specified by the logico-experimental requirement imposed on its answers. Justification, so defined, constitutes the second level of the scientific enterprise; to put it more adequately, it is already a determinate problem within the whole questioning process called science. It is a problem that has its specified rules of resolution, and it requires that nothing problematic remain in the final product if the difference between questions and answers is to prevail, as it should. The problem constituted by justification is to suppress all the problems which were initially raised by answering them.

3. LOGICISM VERSUS PSYCHOLOGISM

The major problem for us concerns the formation of science: how does it progress? How are results acquired? In our terms, how does the scientist proceed from questions to answers, and what does it mean to have an answer in science?

For positivism, the answers to all these questions are clear and are based upon the following *a priori:* everything that matters to the epistemologist occurs at the level of (logico-experimental) justification. Research, authentic research, is reducible to justification procedures, and, as such, it is a matter of logic and experience. The logic of research is that used in the justificatory process, i.e., formal or classical logic as we can find it in ordinary textbooks on the subject. Research, which covers discovery *and* justification, is identified with the latter by positivists on account of the rationality inherent in science. It is significant that Popper, for example, called *The Logic of Scientific Discovery* (original title: *Logik der Forschung*) what amounts to an analysis of justification procedures, reducing the whole of scientific activity to its final stage in order to make the latter rational right through. *This implies that no other type of rationality, save the one defined by classical logic, is entitled to existence.*

To this restrictive view, one has found opposed an idea of research strictly based on psychological factors: chance, intuition, inspiration, genius, association of ideas, etc. Justification deals with results (which have already been discovered at a prior stage of inquiry), but with it alone one cannot explain how they have been found, since it leaves in the shadow how they were discovered. Justification, therefore, does not bring anything new in science. Though this last point is undoubtedly true, psychologism suffers from the defect of seeing discovery as a mere subjective process, devoid of any rational and objective component. If rationality refuses to be reduced solely to the laws of classical logic, as logicism would like, it cannot be absent, however, from discovery as if chance or intuition were *the* factors of progress. One can hardly see how science could ever be rationally acquired, nor extended, if it were restricted to either subjective components or logical rearrangements of results. Logicism focused on the logic of the second level of the global research process and denied that there was an intrinsic logic ruling the first level, or that such a level could exist at all, equating it with the second when not simply denying it. As to psychologism, it only saw the subjective component of the first level to which it reduced synthesis and failed to see what was rational in it. In a second phase, logicists as well as psychologists noticed how untenable their narrowed conception was, and they conceded the existence of a double level—positivists even labeled them *discovery* and *justification* (Hans Reichenbach, Carnap, Popper)—although both stages remained completely ignored as the dimensions of a questioning process. Logicism, which eventually realized that science could not be amalgamated with an accumulation of results, admitted that there was a first level (though purely psychological, and therefore illogical), which was, as such, of no concern to the philosopher. The context of justification only should be the subject of a *rationale Nachkonstruktion* (Reichenbach). But logicists seemed to have realized too that they had introduced irrationality at the basis of science; hence Popper's *transference principle*, which abolishes the difference

so grudgingly conceded: *"what is true in logic is true in psychology."*
This enabled him to avoid the disastrous implication of admitting irrationalism as the basis of science. John Stuart Mill, on the other hand, conflated the logic of discovery and the logic of justification into *one* single
logical process (since science obeys logical, i.e., rational, laws) namely,
induction. His goal was to substitute induction for deduction as the true
justificatory procedure. This, of course, is a logicist attitude which is
bound to fail, to the extent that inductive arguments do not possess the
same logical force as their deductive counterparts. At best, induction is
"psychologically valid" (Hume), but it cannot serve as a logical description of discovery substitutable for justification in order to account for
the logic of science.

Let us make it clear that justification, too, is in part subjective. It takes
as much "intuition" to make discoveries as it does to find the appropriate
means to demonstrate their validity. It is most unlikely that someone to
whom the axioms and the allowed rules of inferences of the theory of
natural numbers might be submitted would automatically deduce the
theorems of arithmetic without a good deal of inspiration.

Neither can it be denied that there exists a level prior to justification
which, though subjective, is not merely so. The scientist poses the problems to be solved by linking them together rationally. The history of
science shows that scientists never ask their questions at random, nor do
they formulate them in just any way. Scientists seem to obey a logic
appropriate to the connection of problems, which is, without doubt,
different from the logic applied to answers. Why should we postulate
that the latter is logic itself, and reject, as illogical, all other forms of
rationality?

4. THE LEVELS OF QUESTIONING AND THEIR ARTICULATION

The scientist certainly does not ask right from the start all the questions
he is going to solve during the research process and then answer them
all simultaneously. Beyond the logical distinction between questions and
answers inherent in the very notion of the questioning process, we
should take into account the dynamics of questioning, in which questions and answers succeed one another. Borrowing the terminology
from the Freudian theory, let us call the logical description *topographical* and the second *dynamical.* The former considers questions and
answers as logically distinct, as a static difference, while the latter re-

gards the difference as structural, insofar as questions and answers constantly interact in time. Since questions and answers differ in nature, different laws apply to them, even if there are structural laws to explain their dynamical relationship. The transition from one question to another requires the mediation of an answer at some stage of the process if a synthesis is to take place. Otherwise, the scientist would keep on asking questions without ever attaining answers, and, as a result, the succession of questions would imply no new knowledge but would consist in the duplication of the initial problem. But even during the passage from this initial problem to the final solution, the topographical difference, being constitutive, has to be respected, if questioning is to be at all. Even if a single linguistic expression ceases to be problematic (or hypothetical) and becomes justified as a right and true answer, the moment at which it was questionable, and was actually questioned, and the moment at which it was an answer differ: that same expression was considered differently at both moments. This is the materialization of the topographical difference within the actual questioning process. On the other hand, questions must embody a lack of completeness which can only be suppressed by the answers corresponding to them; otherwise, *answers* would not ensue when *questions* are raised. This factor will be found in the very logic of discovery conceived as a logic of questions.

What are the main implications of the topographical hypothesis?

First, there is a level at which the questioner raises his questions, different from the level at which he establishes his answers, and both levels pertain to the questioning process.

Second, questions form a sequence that is a *logical* order, as do answers. The problems solved by questions disappear as such once they have found their answers; this explains why results are only expounded to the other scientists of the community. The aim of raising problems is to find their solution; they are, therefore, never mentioned and disappear at the level of what is explicit.

Finally, the level of answers represents a network of statements previously discovered, which have been successfully tested and logically arranged (I have called that *justification,* in a loose sense of the word). This is what counts as an answer in science.

How does the transition from questions to answers take place? If we assume that the questioner proceeds from question to question, merely dynamizing the topographical difference, and finally answers them, then we should conclude that he does not progress at all at the questions level, nor would he at the answers level, since justification does not bring about new results but operates with those which have already been found. Where do the successive problems come from, if nothing unproblematical underlies them, if no answer directs the ongoing research toward a further question? The research process, like a tire on ice, would then turn without gripping. Whence the second possibility.[4] The questioner proceeds from question to answer, each answer sustaining the research (for as long as the initial problem is not solved) by being itself a new question or, at least, by giving rise to one. Each answer is but a step in the whole process, and each expresses a new question by not being the final answer which brings the inquiry to an end. That is why they are entitled to be called *problematological*: they are partial answers, which are not the answers sought for, in the sense that they refer back to the questions they express and to those they give rise to. They do not count as answers for the questioner, since the answers which can bear that name for him do not allude any more to the research process, i.e., to the questions, but are self-sufficient and autonomous with respect to the latter. They are free from any problematicity, since the initial problem (and those conditioned by it within the process) has been solved through them and disappears as such. Nonetheless, problematological answers solve partially what has been asked at the outset. The term *problematological* indicates that the answers under consideration keep the scientific questioning open and that it must be pursued. Logico-experimental validation is itself a problem within the whole process, a problem which the questioner must eventually face. As a result, we can look upon the research process as made up of problematological answers. The inquiry is completed when the last answer is found, which remains, in this sense, conjectural: any answer referring back to a question, because of its being an answer, is, as such, problematological too.

Of course, this is but one aspect of the whole description, to the extent that we have been leaving aside the topographical requirements, in virtue of which answers, as such, should have nothing to do with questions if they actually solve them. In other words, the fact that the questioner moves from a question to an answer which, as such, solves his problem compels us to see in this transition something other than a mere continuum of problematological answers. Each answer put forth to solve a question is a solution by itself because it is an *answer,* not merely an assertoric repetition of the question. With respect to the question solved, the answer is not problematological, even if it is problematological (= expressing a problem) in reference to what lies ahead. With respect to the question solved, the answer is *apocritical,* whereas it is problematological with respect to the one it gives rise to. The word ἀπόκρισις means *answer* in Greek. An apocritical answer is therefore one which does not express a question, which has even nothing to do with questions, apart from the fact that it emerged from the necessity of solving one of them. The apocritical answer may be viewed, nonetheless, as referring back to questions, but only as that which suppresses them, since they no longer need to be raised. The reference is implicit, and exterior to the statement serving as an answer: its being an *answer* does not appear explicitly in it, but belongs to the process in which the statement originated. The apocritical features of science are logic and experience. Consequently, the characteristic of the apocritical answer is that it is not put forth *as* an answer (that it is not situated in reference to a determinate question), but as something which only says what it has to say. It is *valid* and is so independently of what it originated from. It is referential, not of a question, but of some objectual content; it states something in particular and nothing else. What is in question may be seen in the statement itself, or through it, but is not affirmed by it. There is no reference in any way to the question which brought about the *production* of the statement, because the object of the answer is not to speak about itself and the condition of its emergence. Its answerhood falls outside what it states, i.e., outside itself, and falls within the questioning process which is the locus of answerhood. The transition from questions to answers therefore transforms problematological answers into apocritical ones by means of ad hoc logico-experimental procedures. Some of these problematological answers are eliminated or undergo an assertoric transformation, but the expressions which are alternatively problematological and apocritical are one and the same: the research process can *also* (but not exclusively in a question-view of science) be conceived as one of enduring validation. Each question leads to a new answer, and an answer means, in science, a justified statement. The questioner endeavors to ascertain the validity of a proposition by checking to see that its opposite cannot be retained as true. Experience, through experiments and observation, as well as logic, yields that result. Let us give an example: Max Weber sought to demonstrate that the Protestant ethic was determining in the spread of capitalism. Since this question was raised, the possibility of the truth of the opposite judgment had to be considered, in order to validate the original hypothesis. We can trace Weber's analyses of other religions, which did not foster a capitalistic attitude, to his wish to suppress the problematic character of his own proposition (i.e., the alternative). The determination of causes obeys a similar attitude, and is but a particular case of the practice which consists in eliminating irrelevant factors. If I ask a question X, I wish to know whether X is the case, and this implies that X might not be the case:

alternative answers are embodied in my questioning, and its aim is to reach one answer, the answer, and as a result to suppress the alternative possibilities initially raised. This, of course, supposes that the questioner has reached the stage at which experience can be questioned with a yes-or-no query, and that is only possible after a succession of questions which isolate the relevant factors from the irrelevant ones. Yes-or-no questions are, from this point of view, the most decisive ones. Technical apparatus is often built up for that purpose. Let us give an example drawn from the natural sciences.[5] Semmelweis, asking the question of the origin of puerperal fever, put foward the problematological answer, according to which infectious materials were the cause. In order to verify the problematological answer and to make it apocritical, Semmelweis simply divided the women to be cured into two groups, one of them being taken care of by doctors who had washed their hands in a solution destroying the infectious materials. The experiment proved conclusive, the hypothesis was retained, and further research ensued. Each answer is both problematological and apocritical; each is not, as Popper claims, a *mere* conjecture, but is also a result. This phenomenon is captured by classical terminology, wherein questioning is absent, with the key word *hypothesis.* A hypothesis is both a conjecture, whence its problematological character, and an assertion, which is uttered because the questioner assumes it to be true.

The logical difference between question and answer is absent from the notion of hypothesis, which conflates both dimensions as if they were of no relevance to the study of knowledge. Hypotheses are results, too; consequently, what motivates the questioner to put forth a hypothesis can very often be identified as that which justifies it, i.e., the data making it scientifically acceptable.

The interest of devising a peculiar terminology (with such unfamiliar words as *problematological* and *apocritical*) in order to apprehend the reality of the questioning process lies in the following facts. First, when we answer questions posed about questioning we should be careful not to lose the specificity of questions; that is why *our* answers which denote the questions we speak of, and *our* answers which refer to answers in general, should be marked off. We called the latter apocritical and the former problematological. Second, we have to take into account all the implications of the topographical (or logical) description, which are not limited to a simple matter of terminology imposed by a reflexive level of analysis. Because of the logical difference between question and answer, what is problematological (i.e., a question) and apocritical (i.e., an answer) cannot possess this double property with respect to one and the same question: it is impossible for an answer to be both the explicit expression of a problem and its solution. Third, our terminology allows us to mingle the dynamical description of questioning with the topographical. When we say that a questioner proceeds from a question to an answer, and reciprocally, we mean that he proceeds from a question to a problematological answer, which is also, as an answer, apocritical. Since the question is itself a problematological expression, this implies that he infers an apocritical answer from another one, but also that he derives a problematological answer from a previous one. Because of the topographical difference, answers which have been successively produced as apocritical need to be rearranged in a distinct logical order wherein only answers *qua* judgments appear, this time independently of the questions which gave birth to them. The elaboration of this network of judgments belongs to the dynamical moment labeled *context of justification,* to which validation and observation also pertain, even if the result of this elaboration has nothing dynamical in it and thus stops the process.

Consequently, whether we conceive research as an endless problematological process, which embraces all the problematological answers, or as an apocritical chain amounts ultimately to the same thing, in the sense that one cannot make the first description without being logically committed to the second. Answers refer to questions, and vice versa; as to problematological entities, they are also apocritical, and vice versa, though not in reference to the same thing. This fact necessarily reflects the difference, among answers, between those which are situated in the context of discovery, wherein further questions need to be posed, and those which belong to justification. Considered from a dynamical point of view, apocritical answers refer to a problematological level which is different: they are answers, and that is all. Topographically speaking they are just truths, logically ordered, and they are presented as judgments. And these only appear at the explicit level. Indeed, the scientist is only interested in the results; as a scientist, he does not care to know how a colleague has come to them. The scientist, if he were to look upon science from a scientist's point of view, would necessarily adopt the topographical standpoint. Questioning is a process, hence a dynamic, and so a scientist would not see answers in his results, but mere results. His topographical standpoint, by not being supplemented with the dynamical one, would not be based on an approach through questioning, but on statements. Whence the temptation, for the philosopher, to investigate science as if it were only a universe of results and judgments, failing to discover behind the apocritical level of science what, in it, indicates that it comes from the problematological. This temptation must be resisted if the philosopher of science is to avoid the pitfalls of positivism.

The questioner advances by asking questions, for perceiving a problem already constitutes a synthesis and formulating it adds new presuppositions to the existing theory. This discovery is therefore an answer, but a problematological one. It must be tested, and as long as it is not (successfully) validated, it can at best be counted as a partial answer to the initial problem (which remains so). The "results" constituted by the array of problematological answers are not results for the questioner, who must keep on questioning. These answers, because they partially solve the initial problem, are nonetheless answers. They are apocritical with respect to the questions which, at each step, gave rise to them. The discoveries are progressively justified; it would be senseless to pursue an inquiry without securing firm bases. This, of course, does not rule out, but even implies, that investigating a particular problem is done by taking up easier (sub)questions.

Because an apocritical answer becomes autonomous with respect to its conditions of emergence, it may be problematological of another problem yet to arise and, as a consequence, of a new questioning process defined by that new problem. A scientific result can always be incorporated into a new process where it becomes "alive" (or generative) again.[6] The term *problematological,* applied to answers, means that the expression under consideration acts either as a partial solution to a problem other than the one initially solved, that it expresses the new problem, or even that it *allows* the latter to be solved. An answer is apocritical with respect to the question it solves, and problematological to the problem it asks, which must evidently differ. This terminology enables us to show that answers are not the totally autonomous results to which positivists used to reduce science, since they are also problematological (though they are not so in relationship to what they answer), nor are they mere conjectures, as Popper claims. They would be *solely* problematological, and this would contradict their being answers. On the other hand, the apocritical answers are not found together as a whole, and they do not automatically put themselves into a logical sequence. They undergo a final treatment in which they are ordered, as is described by the topographical analysis. The very notion of apocritical answer captures both the dynamical and topographical implications. An answer which is apocritical is also an answer and, as such, refers back to some question; an answer which is apocritical appears as a mere truth, having nothing to do with what is problematic.

The problematological feature of answers is therefore absent. This affirmation is not contradictory to the earlier analysis of apocritical answers, which was *dynamical;* the one just given represents the *topographical* viewpoint. The topographical difference is a moment of the dynamic of questioning. The necessity of a topographical arrangement of answers within the dynamic of questioning into a logically autonomous and distinct level springs from the need to dissociate the answers from the questions, i.e., to detach the former from a particular *process.* Problematological answers are not identical to apocritical answers, solely because they are considered differently from two points of view. An answer found during the context of discovery is considered problematological, even if it comes to be realized later as apocritical in the context of justification. This kind of answer is envisaged as the expression of a question. This new question undoubtedly marks progress and therefore is an answer, but in the course of discovery it is not viewed as an apocritical one, even if it turns out to be so. Were the answer to be regarded as belonging to the ultimate results of the research process, then it would not be seen as a contribution to further discoveries but as a piece of established and unquestionable knowledge. In consequence, the questioner moves from question to question and, by so doing, answers the former; but these answers only become such on a second level where the rearrangement of the results found takes place. From the dynamical point of view, discovery and justification are interwoven in time and form two logically distinct contexts; but the topographical analysis requires more than that: the answers, which are mingled with the questions, do not count as real answers as long as they are not autonomized into a distinct *level.* This arrangement occurs, within the dynamical process, in the context of justification. This presenting of the results is that which brings the process to an end. In other words, at the first level, the problematological answers are not answers *for the questioner,* as to the apocritical answers, they do not refer back to questions, whence their apparently autonomous character, apparent to the extent that autonomy is itself relative to the process from which it results. Philosophy of science restricted to its topographical tracing would evidently fail to see what science has to do with questioning. The autonomy of answers, on our view, is perfectly captured when we say that any answer is both apocritical *and* problematological (see Chapter 4), since an answer is not merely so in reference to what it has solved, but is also an answer with respect to other questions. The original problem *was,* but *is* no longer, and it is replaced by a statement, its solution.

5. THE LOGIC OF DISCOVERY AS LOGIC OF THE PROBLEMATOLOGICAL LEVEL

One of the consequences of what has been said in the preceding section is that a solution put forth in answer to a theoretical problem constitutes an answer *with regard to* the theory: either it accepts the presuppositional horizon the theory represents or it puts it explicitly into question (as the person who answers that there is no king of France to the question of knowing whether or not he is bald). But since there exists a structural difference between what comes under the heading of a problem and what comes under the heading of solution, a new theoretical solution to a problem in terms of a given theory is possible without it being necessary to place oneself within and to accept this horizon of presuppositions.[7]

Rationality consists in solving problems. Knowing how to state them usefully is already a rational enterprise. A technical problem, such as the construction of a bridge, implements the appropriate rationality, and a rational solution is one which permits the construction of the bridge. And so it is for all problems. A scientific problem requires the application of logico-experimental procedures which bestow on the answers found during the course of the research the status of answers *for* the questioning process. As shown earlier, the link between questions and their answers is meaning. The logic which governs the transition from the successive problems to the partial answers is therefore a logic of meaning. On the other hand, it is a logic of assertion which links together the answers which have already been proven—mathematical logic, propositional logic, and predicate logic. The answers refer but to themselves, they are answers which conceal their answer-ness and appear as simple, logically connected judgments.

The logic characteristic of the problematological level is one of meaning, since the transition from one question to another requires the intermediary of an answer. The context, represented both by science at large and by the subjectivity of the questioner, is a determining factor. The transition from questions to answers is, at first, one to answers which for the scientist are not answers, so long as they have not been justified and arranged in an autonomous order of exposition. They are answers insofar as they add to the knowledge of the questioner, who performs thereby a true synthesis. Each question which is asked adds, not by what it says, but by what it presupposes, to the tacit knowledge contained in the question which precedes it. The succession of questions forms a set of problematological answers which, if we choose to express them, to clarify them, to say what they add to the preceding result, will become apocritical with respect to the *reflexive* questioning process. For the scientific questioning process, no problematological answer is totally autonomous, so long as the initial problem remains unsolved and is displaced as such through the successive subquestions. But each of these questions can only come into being if the preceding question has been resolved, and its result becomes a stepping-stone to the next question. This result, presupposed by each successive question, and so on until the logico-experimental verification has been completed, is therefore an answer which must become apocritical not for a reflexive process but only *with respect to the scientific process which gave birth to it.*

Which conditions must this logic of the problematological level satisfy?

First, it must be characterized by the fact that the accession to the new problematological answers modifies somewhere the *meaning* of some *terms,* as they are found in preceding theories and answers. The meaning is the link between the questions and the answers, and the answers act as stepping-stones between the questions.

Second, it must embody a lack of completeness which demands to be suppressed, a gap which needs to be filled by the apocritical level, where the meaning of the terms is necessarily and unambiguously fixed. The demand constituted by the first level must reveal an enigma and must be understood as such. Hence the basic features of the first level: problematicity, and the need to suppress it through a second level, complementary to the first.

Finally, the opportunity for routine discovery must exist in the very structure of the logic of that first level. Synthesis can then fall back on knowledge which has already been acquired by science at large. If the questioner learns something with the answer given to him or found by him, it in no way implies that his synthesis is a synthesis with regard to the global corpus. It is the absence of this distinction between routine synthesis and global synthesis in the various philosophies of discovery that gave rise to the controversy involving Karl Popper and Thomas S. Kuhn.

Popper,[8] according to Kuhn, makes no distinction between normal, everyday science and science in a state of revolution. He does not differentiate between those problems which make science progress globally and those which advance only the knowledge of the questioner. In consequence, how can one distinguish between that synthesis which truly increases scientific knowledge and that which limits itself to drawing conclusions from an existing problematic without renewing or extending it?[9] Popper justly replies that the innovative or revolutionary solution of problems, in Kuhn, undergoes a radical qualitative jump which makes questioning *qua* synthesis impossible, since all scientists of the "ancien régime" would be precluded from having access to the "revolutionary conquests." In Popper, synthesis *qua* revolution does not make sense, since problem solving is supposed to put us immediately into contact with new truths. Kuhn versus Popper—impossible questioning (as innovative synthesis for science at large) versus useless questioning. We recognize here the old paradox of Plato (*Meno,* 80e), applied to scientific questioning, to synthesis in science.

To change meanings, to bring about equivocality by working out new senses of old terms which partially keep their former meaning, or, to put it otherwise, to create enigmas which are semantical, is called *metaphorization.* The metaphorical process, as described by most specialists, fulfills exactly the three conditions of the logic of the problematological level. The logic of discovery is metaphorizaton,[10] but this does not imply that it is only made up of metaphors; nor does it mean that the whole problematological level is made up of metaphors, because this would render it unintelligible. There may be metonymies, for example, among many other substitutional forms. The characteristic of the problematological level is that it brings into play expressions which are *substituted* for the basic problem that research is trying to solve, *though they add to it.* They are all equivalent in that they shift the emphasis away from the basic problem: it is this problem which gives the signification of the succession of problematological answers. One and the same meaning, yet, pervades the level. But there would be no progression if the basic problem were shifted by each problematological answer *without* any alteration of meaning. The phenomenon of the conservation and modification of meaning is what we usually call the "metaphorical process": A is B and not B,[11] without there being any contradiction. The assertion therefore cannot be taken literally: its exact meaning, which makes it univocal, lies elsewhere, and it is this meaning which is given by the problem.

We consequently understand the central role of the hermeneutic in the sciences, which did not escape the attention of such philosophers as Gadamer or Emilio Betti. In the first moment of the transition from questions to answers, the answer obtained, like the basic question, is problematological; for this very reason, it is not an answer for the questioner who reached it. The problem expressed is one and the same, thus permitting the substitution of one problematological answer for another. But the identity of meaning denotes the difference: a difference of contents, a nonequivalence between what is said in the two statements.

Each of the problematological answers, *qua* answers, says something different. If they were the answers sought in the last analysis by the questioner, if they represented his solution, they would merely be contradictions asserting literally incompatible contents. Problematological answers create new shifts in meaning on the basis of old definitions, and they present as identical what is not so. Hence, they often demand to be replaced by an *answer,* which, *strictly speaking,* suppresses the conflation, because answers declare what they state without explicitly stipulating their relationship to the questions from which they originated: they are world oriented. This suppression is, of course, one of the basic features of science. In poetry, metaphors remain what they are; in science, where conformity to reality is an essential requirement, metaphors must disappear to give way to clear and univocal concepts. Otherwise, there would not be any difference between mere category-mistakes or insane speech, and scientific creativity. The existence of a second level grounds the difference between madness, in which metaphorical speech is taken literally as being the true picture of reality, and creativity in science, which submits itself to the sense of reality and the requirements of experience.

Hence, a new substitution forces itself when the problematological answer is metaphorical—that of an answer to the enigma represented by the metaphorical propositions, which suppresses it or disambiguates it if no preexistent terminology is available. It may seem rather odd, at first sight, to view metaphors as enigmas or questions. Is "Richard is a lion" a question? Strictly speaking, this is not an interrogative sentence, and there is no need to give any answer to the person who utters that metaphor. Nonetheless, we should be careful not to commit what I would call the *assertoric fallacy,* which consists in isolating sentences out of the context of their utterance and in seeing them as autonomous and self-sufficient products, analyzable per se. A metaphor requires a context in order to be understood; taken in itself, unless it is already a cliché, it is an enigma which can only be resolved by appeal to the process which gave rise to it and which puts the metaphor within a given situation. As Aristotle said (*Poetics,* 1458a), metaphorical discourse requires a nonmetaphorical context, i.e., a knowledge which is not itself in question.

On the contrary, the interrogative model of science does not deny the role of intuition in discovery. Science progresses by asking questions and answering them, and even if we were to make the whole process the result of inspiration it would not alter the fact that results, wherever and however they arise, are so in virtue of their being answers to questions. In fact, the role of intuition and subjectivity becomes manifest when the metaphorical event takes place by the bringing together of the terms of the metaphor. Once the "right" enigma is found, that is to say, once the right manner of stating the basic problem has been discovered, the logic of the process follows an objective course. A problematological answer, which metaphorizes the basic problem, is substituted for it, and the metaphor must then be eliminated in order *to achieve univocity.* A nonproblematic meaning arises from the substitution for one that already exists, i.e., a declarative sentence stating a proposition belonging to the scientific corpus. The synthesis of the first level disappears at the second level: if I say, for example, "King Richard is a lion," I have not made a discovery, since what I say is already known to the historians, namely, that Richard is (a) courageous (king). Nonetheless, there is resolution of a problem in such a situation too, even if the knowledge so produced increases the understanding of the questioner only: Richard is x, as the lion is x. The judgment "Richard is a lion" derives from the synthesis in Diagram 1 where x represents the set of courageous beings. The predicative aspect of the x's can also be looked into, for nothing proves that we must take the *extensional* point of view. "Being x" signifies, then, "being courageous." The metaphorization synthesizes three predicates into two. This results in a judgment. In the present example, it is an existential one: $(\exists x)(Rx.Lx)$. The characteristic of the synthesis of the metaphorical process is that it subsumes individuals who have nothing in common (i.e., no known predicates) under a common concept, to be invented (or to be found). The questioning can go on: either one tries to see if the x's, which are P, have other properties, R, S, ... that individuals who are Q already possess, or one tries to see if individuals other than those who are P are also x because they have already similar properties. The metaphor "P is Q" then suggests variations both of the predicates and subjects, for P and Q can, indifferently, express both ("P is Q" can signify "x is P, x is Q," for example). And by starting from the subjects one can then proceed to a study of their properties. It is in this way that the properties of light analogous to those of sound were sought—on the basis of properties common to both "substances."[12] Or, on the basis of the discovery of common properties, other "substances" could have been sought to which these properties might have been applied (sound, light, gas, etc.).

The metaphor refers to a referent *as* being this or that. No object can be separated from the manner in which it is given: it *is,* insofar as it is this or that. The metaphor leads the questioner to see to what degree the subject of his metaphor *is* this or that. The fact that metaphorization is both an intensional and an extensional process clearly indicates that we

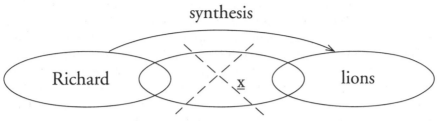

Diagram 1.

cannot isolate what in it is referential and what derives solely from the analysis of predicates. What is metaphorical relates its description of objects to something else, either objects or predicates. This other reality is the presupposition of the metaphor, and it is not itself metaphorical. It serves as the background for the understanding of the new, even if what is new is irreducible to the existing body of scientific knowledge. The presence of a metaphorical enigma leads the questioner to look for an equivalent nonmetaphorical meaning. If he cannot find it in the existing body of science, science at large increases, since the questioner must take into account the irreducible newness of experience; *irreducible* means here that something already found cannot be substituted to what is new, not that the bridges between the old and the new are irreducibly burned. The metaphorization which brings something really new to science at large must find a nonmetaphorical translation or definition, which established knowledge cannot provide alone, even though it allows us to understand the metaphor. A nonmetaphorical proposition cannot be substituted here for the metaphor, which must be kept as such. How, then, does the scientist deal with it? Either he focuses on the referent to see if it possesses the same properties as its *analogon* or he focuses on the properties of an already known referent. He then can recognize new objects and new properties. Or he can proceed to the apocritical stage of his inquiry.

All this, of course, is somewhat simplified here; my point is to show how metaphorization covers what we mean by logic of discovery. For fuller understanding, it would be necessary to study in greater detail the extensional and intensional aspects of the metaphor and then to investigate the problem of the possible relationship between the triadic structures of the metaphor and the syllogism.

However, in the remainder of this chapter I shall confine myself to the question of the relationship between metaphorization and logical-experimental validation.

A metaphor either refers to an absent property or suggests the possibility of an identity between individuals sharing known properties. In the first case, one tries to discover the property which fits (Richard is a lion → Richard is courageous) and to find, or at the very least, define it with the help of those properties presupposed by the second term of the metaphor (here, "the lion"). It is this property which makes a metaphor like "Richard is a lion" univocal. In the second case, one tries to see if all or any of the properties which apply to the first type of individuals apply, strictly speaking, to the second. These operations, which respond to the metaphorical enigma, are logical-experimental in nature. They do away with the metaphor by putting forth a precise and univocal meaning. The metaphor irreducible to existing scientific knowledge can be kept as it is; but that knowledge which is presupposed by different predicates applies to the terms of the metaphor and grants to it a new meaning which no individual term possesses. The metaphor acquires a nonmetaphorical meaning by making explicit the implicit properties whose applicability to reality gives rise to verification. The questioner, on the other hand, led on by a metaphor, may attempt to find a new formulation and, thus, give up the original metaphor. He creates a new definition by ascribing, for example, a conventional "name" to the property in question. This procedure also belongs to the logical-experimental validation, i.e., logical rearrangement and the presentation of new definitions. The questioner will give unambiguous expression to the "image" he first had, an expression which ultimately validates the metaphorical image.

One must therefore distinguish between irreducible (or revolutionary) and ordinary (everyday) research: the first increases science at large, while the second takes place within a theoretical problematic whose presuppositions have been validated earlier and are now extended. In addition to the point of view of science at large, the questioner's viewpoint must be considered too. If he already had the answer to his questions, he would not ask them; consequently, whether science at large progresses or not by the putting forth of an answer, we are justified in asserting that, at the very least, it increases the knowledge of the questioner. From his point of view a synthesis has taken place: it is a *primary* synthesis if it increases science at large; it is *secondary* (or derivative) if it retains the questioner within the realm of existing scientific knowledge (through deduction, for example).

This classification allows us to understand a fact which has long troubled mathematical philosophers in particular—namely, that analytic (Kant), deductive (Mill), or tautological judgments (Frege, Wittgenstein) can increase knowledge. But what kind of knowledge? If we do not distinguish between the various points of view, as I was led to do earlier in the discussion concerning both Popper and Kuhn, or later about metaphors, an insurmountable difficulty appears: a set of formal and analytic truths, verbally expressed, supposed to increase knowledge will, in fact, not do so. Much of our sciences would not teach anybody anything at all. In reality, analytic discourse helps present the results and reveal the deductive relationships characteristic of justification. They are therefore supposed to teach someone something, even if they only crystallize the discoveries already made. They no longer increase knowledge at large (of which they, being analytic, are but a part), but they do increase the knowledge of all those to whom they are addressed—i.e., the scientific community, made up of scientists and students who are questioners other than the discoverer. Thanks to the identity criterion I suggested earlier, it can be seen that a questioner may quite easily be unaware that a given question is identical with another and that an answer to a question he does not ask also answers a question he does ask. If he does not ask the first question, it may be because he already knows the answer to it. By making the right substitutions, this answer may lead to the answer he is in fact looking for. A bridge is thus set up between what he knows and what he does not know, and networks of analytic judgments which link a proposition of personal knowledge with a proposition of global knowledge may come into existence. This is how analytic judgments can increase knowledge while, at the same time and from another angle, they do not do so. By not considering scientific judgments in their context, which includes an interlocutor to whom they are addressed, we can only foresee the rebirth of the sterile opposition between the inductivists and the deductivists, between the partisans of Mill and P. W. Bridgman, on the one side, and those of Carl Hempel, on the other.

Conclusion:
What Is Problematology?

1. QUESTIONING AS A NEW FOUNDATION

In philosophy, the first question to
ask is that of what is first. By such a query, we have to understand the
question of what should be considered as the foundation of thought, its
principle. Since we cannot presuppose anything in philosophy, we must
accept having only that very question at our disposal in order to reach
the answer. What is originary in the question of the originary, if not the
question itself? The principle of thought is therefore questioning. Even if
we call that principle into question, we are still questioning, thereby
verifying the principle.

Traditionally, as we have seen in the preceding chapters, the foundation of philosophy has been associated with Being, and, later, with human subjectivity (or consciousness). These interpretations of the first
answer to the question of principle suffer from the same defect: they do
not take into consideration the fact that they result from an act of questioning and that, therefore, they are answers. An answer which claims to
be originary without affirming the primacy of questioning cannot be
first; it would always presuppose the question to which it is the answer,

an act of interrogation which is actually primary. An answer which affirms something other than questioning as the first principle of thought would presuppose the negation of questioning as a norm. The eradication of alternatives can be called the research of necessity, but as a research it cannot appear as such—necessity must necessarily be asserted right from the start as a necessity. A principle of necessity which is itself apodictic must contain its own necessity by itself; God has played that role, the *cogito* and consciousness too, but at the time of the Greeks it was Being. How could Being be other than being, i.e., what it is? What is must essentially be itself.

In any event, whatever answer has been offered on the identity of the absolute foundation of thought is one which can never reflect its own answerhood. It must be a statement, a proposition, a first truth enunciated as such, as a starting point. The intuition of that starting point must impose itself as such, logically, ontologically, discursively, mentally. Throughout history, two main groups of first principles have emerged, those which rather favor the subject and those which give privilege to the object—idealism or realism, in sum. Questioning is then understood either as a characteristic of man or as always referring to some piece of the external world. Let us consider the two possibilities.

As a human activity with an object, questioning cannot be autonomous. The question of what comes first, the question of questioning, then disappears in the question of man, or, if we prefer the other alternative, the question of reality (or of Being). The difficulty which we find in that traditional reductionism is this: How can we speak of man and the world without questioning them in some way or other? In other words, How can we find an answer on what is considered to be the first principle without questioning it first? And if we do, does it not prove the (more) originary nature of questioning in that matter? If to philosophize is to think without presupposition, the question of man or of Being cannot but refer to questioning as the only "presupposition." If, for example, man is considered the ultimate and true beginning or foundation of thought, the position must be questioned in order to be stated and subsequently analyzed, and we fall back on the priority of questioning.

Propositionalism, in its realistic or idealistic ontologies, has always reduced the question of principle to the norm it purported to establish. The propositionality of its query has always amounted to abolishing that very quest as such, and thereby has served as the model of answerhood and the reason not to reflect it as such. We still all bear in mind the Cartesian procedure, for instance, which exemplifies that procedure of eradication. If everything is called into doubt, everything is questionable, including that very assertion and, indeed, assertability at large. Nothing is certain; nothing can escape radical doubt. If Descartes had been consistent, he should have stopped with this affirmation, but he did not. He claimed that the *expression* of doubt (i.e., doubt) is itself an apodictic truth, as if it were distinct from doubt itself. In other words, to doubt is not to question, as we could have thought it was, but it is already to assert some statement. To doubt is to affirm that one doubts. As such, it is a statement which is out-of-the-question, as if radical doubt were not really some radical questioning, but already the apodictic answer to some original question which is suppressed by virtue of the simple fact that it has been raised. To doubt is to *say* that one doubts, it is thought affirming itself apodictically, apodicticity being thereby considered as the principle for the whole *logos,* in sum, its guiding norm.

Questioning has to be affirmed to exist at all, but propositionalism makes it disappear in that very affirmation, which therefore renders it literally impossible, if not as a modality of assertability at large.

Problematology, on the other hand, aims at keeping alive the difference between questioning and answering. It does so in order to avoid making the former a modality of the latter, thereby suppressing the difference in some self-developing propositional order. We need a different language for questioning and answering, or at least we need a language in which the difference can be expressed.

2. LANGUAGE, THOUGHT, AND FICTION

We often think by reflecting on the problems we have in mind, and we often respond by speaking, i.e., by offering answers. The implicit and the explicit represent the most obvious modality of differentiation, but it is not the only one. We may have to express our problems, if the problem we have in mind must be solved by somebody else. Form, here, plays a major role. It enables both the locutor and the audience to indicate or identify what is problematic and what is not. When the context is sufficiently clear on that matter, form will play a lesser role: the context will be the problematological marker (or differentiator) between question and answer.

In literature, for instance, we observe a diminished role of the context, as if the text had to create its own environment (auto-contextualization). The difference between what is in question and what is not must be found in the text itself. Form, therefore, will have an essential role. The more explicit the problem, the more referential the text is, and the reader finds himself all the closer to a situation of everyday life, with its values and presuppositions. The reader is all the more passive: he observes the intrigue unfolding, and participates by his reading in the quest leading to a resolution, as in love or crime stories. Conversely, if the problematic remains implicit, the question of what has initiated the problematic raised by the text is posed to the reader, who is therefore more active and inquisitive. Mimetic reading has given way to a more participatory reception of the text. The latter, in fact, appears all the more enigmatic since the textual answer seems to have enigmaticity itself as its object, as if the goal of the text was to raise some question without expressing it literally. Increased figurativity is coextensive with the increased enigmaticity of the text.

3. THE QUESTION OF MEANING

This question, as we have just seen, is linked with the relationship between questions and answers. What is in question in a given text is identical to the meaning of that text. An answer always evokes the question to which it serves as an answer, even if it does not stipulate "I answer this or that." It also suggests new and different questions. Meaning is shown without always having to be stated at the metalevel. A text *has* a meaning without necessarily *giving* it, and sometimes it must really be sought after (hermeneutics).

When considered as an answer, an opinion, a belief, or a statement can always be questioned afresh. Dialectics or dialogical games ensue from such a possibility, which is nothing but argumentation itself.

The question-answer complex leads to some interesting relations:

1. Its discovery belongs to hermeneutics (for texts) or to semantics (for sentences or statements)
2. Its dismissal actually amounts either to rejecting the question, which is another way of answering it, or to rejecting the answer as being the true one, as being adequate to the problem raised. This defines the field of argumentation

Approbation, too, belongs to argumentation theory, since it is a comment on the link between a question and its proposed answer. Dialectics (or dialogical process) takes place at that level. Locutor and audience

alternate in questioning and answering. Both roles instantiate the problematological difference.

Dialectics, argumentation, and hermeneutics thus pertain to the most
basic features of language use. Even in pragmatics and semantics, we find
questioning at work. Isolated sentences embody terms, such as names
and predicates, which represent deleted interrogatives.

To say something is to offer an answer on a given topic, a certain
question. That question can be misjudged by the locutor, who deems it
solved in the mind of his audience. The question will then reappear and
give rise to a discussion, if not a debate, and the terms used will reveal
their answerhood at the second level of answering. When some statement is uttered, it is already an answer, even when no interrogative
seems present. The problematological difference already manifests itself
in the difference between subject and predicate, where some term enables the locutor to speak of what is in question by means of what is not
(for him).

The subjective aspect of language does not reduce itself to the *dialectical* dimension of language, but includes a *pragmatical* one. The fact of
saying something, of uttering a judgment, is in itself a response to a given
problem, different from what is in question in the content of the judgment, its reference. We fall back here on the old Jakobsonian model,
"sender-message-receiver" or "locutor-discourse-audience" (in Austinian
terms, illocutionary-locutionary-perlocutionary), or on its more metaphysical version, *expression-reference-persuasion.* This structure corresponds to the most basic questions man has addressed since he was on
earth, those of the Self, the World, and the Other. These problems are
embodied here in the linguistic transaction. The three modes of language use are the expressive, the referential, and the rhetorical.

Why is the pragmatico-subjective level of analysis so important in the
determination of meaning? Meaning can be indefinitely pursued: "Napoleon lost at Waterloo" can evoke the question "Who was Napoleon?" The
answer, in turn, can give rise to new questions, if the interlocutor does
not know *who* is the husband of Josephine, *what* a husband is, *who*
Josephine was, and so forth.

At some point, questioning must stop. Understanding relies on a mutual agreement as to the authority and, in the mind of the receiver, the
credibility of what is said.

We can always analyze a statement on the sole basis of *what* is said, of
what is *in question* in it. But the fact of uttering such a statement as a
response or as an expression of a given problem provides an answer on
what is usually called the intention of the locutor. The figurative implica-

tion hidden behind the literal content of what is said depends upon that intentionality. As such, a statement like "Snakes are dangerous" replies to the question of knowing whether x is y, whether the property y (or that which defines the beings we call the y) applies or not. Maybe there are no such x, but uttering the statement indicates that the locutor believes they exist and that they are y. Two questions are then solved by that utterance: (1) there are x which we usually call "snakes," and, if we meet such beings, we must be careful to avoid them; and, (2) such x have the property y.

The negation of the original statement could therefore imply the negation of (1), (2), or both. If we pass by some x which looks like a snake without taking any precaution, it shows that we *either* believe (rightly or wrongly) that x is something else, or that, though being a snake, it is not dangerous, or both. As such, a phrase like "Snakes are dangerous," if considered as a mere statement rather than as an utterance, does not tell us what is in question. Maybe we wish to speak of dangerous creatures, or, on the contrary, we want to address the topic of what snakes may be.

As a result, when we encounter an x which looks like a snake and when we avoid it, our act does prove that we have answered two questions: "What is x?" and "Is this an x?" We implicitly affirm, by our behavior, that we think that snakes are dangerous and that the x encountered is a snake.

Syllogisms emerge as the natural response to the double query embodied in any utterance, and argumentation begins with the discussion of either question. Since every affirmation implies two questions, one on the attribution, the other on the reference, syllogisms must have two premises if a conclusive inference is to be carried out. "Men are mortal" implies that we are able to recognize x as a man; if we come across a given x, we must also be susceptible of ascribing a property that identifies it, from which we can draw other conclusions, apodictic or not.

As noted, argumentation is also related to the double query. We can debate the question of knowing whether (all) snakes are dangerous, accepting that the object seen is a snake, or we could dispute the fact that what we face on our path is really a snake. A statement which would not be considered in its context of utterance, but contemplated as a sheer phrase, would then imply two questions: (1) Can we recognize the x? (2) Do they have the property we assign to them, which permits identification? These questions are embodied in the single act of empirical recognition.

In pragmatics, the question bears on the reason to say what we say. Affirming something means to solve, partially or not, some question. If I

say "Snakes are dangerous," it may be because I have seen one, or because I ask myself what kind of creatures snakes are. We may have seen
something which we have recognized as a snake, and what is *not* in
question is that they are dangerous. Or we may have seen a snake,
beyond any doubt, and then be led to ask whether we should change our
route. The question can also deal with the reason to raise one of those
questions. That question then addresses the problem which lies at the
roots of the utterance; in our example, the question is obviously one of
life and death.

4. THE NATURE OF RHETORIC

Traditionally, rhetoric has been divided into three genres and three main
groups of topics: the deliberative, forensic, and epidictic genres deal,
respectively, with the useful, the just, and the beautiful (i.e., political
rhetoric, legal reasoning, and aesthetical considerations of praise and
blame, pleasure and distantiation). Three aspects intervene in each case:
the role of the locutor (his *ethos*), the affects and emotions of the
audience (*pathos*), and the message itself, which can be more or less
argumentative, or, conversely, more or less ornamental and pleasant, by
virtue of the form of language, as in literary discourse. The Jakobsonian
model is clearly of Aristotelian descent.

   In fact, we face here three types of questions, as has already been
clearly expressed in the *Rhetorica ad Herennium* (I, XI, 18–19). There
are questions of fact, questions of qualification, and questions of reason
or causality. These constitute the most basic types of query, from which
all others ensue. However, they can be conceived on new grounds: the
question of fact bears on the subject, the question of qualification on the
predicate, and the third question on the reason. This way of seeing
rhetoric more or less doubles the syllogistic structure.

   Whatever its form, rhetoric deals with the problematic and the questionable. Manipulative or *evil rhetoric* plays on the unjustified abolition
of something which remains problematic, because it only offers problematic answers. Manipulation and propaganda proceed as if the question
they were dealing with were solved. In contrast, *positive rhetoric* exhibits the questions and puts forth arguments in favor of or against the
chosen solution.

   When seen as based on the use of questioning, rhetoric ceases to be a
"weak" form of reasoning. This view transcends the classical opposition

between the rhetoric of *figures* (or literary rhetoric) and the rhetoric of
conflict (or argumentation, legal or not).

All reasoning implies questions to be addressed, if not solved; at least
they are answered. Logic works only with the answers and their links,
while rhetoric concentrates on the relationship between questions and
answers. That relationship can, but must not, lead to apodicticity. All
answers are on the same footing, and we all know that a contingent,
literary description of some given fact is sometimes "truer" than any
scientific theory.

Literature creates enigmaticity as much as it expresses it. When one
solution is favored, literary discourse gives way to arguments (although
it can also include them). All forms of speech, from literature to legal
procedure, involve questions.

5. SCIENTIFIC REASONING

Rhetoric differs from science and from common sense in the way questions are tackled and answered. Rhetoric is at work in science and in
everyday reasoning, but in a different manner, which is less manifest in
scientific knowledge.

The main feature of commonsense knowledge is the ad hoc character
of the solutions that are favored. Common sense, to that extent, may be
called "opportunistic," an adjective that is the opposite of "systematic"
and "always consistent." Today, we have some ready-made idea at our
disposal; tomorrow, under changed circumstances, we shall resort to
another one. Commonsense responses vary from situation to situation—
the answer tailored to one set of circumstances would most likely fail to
apply to another one. The efficacy of common sense relies on intuition
and observation, stemming from the recurrence of problems in a more
or less stable environment.

Common sense does not test its answers. They are there, so to speak,
at our disposal, received from education, our family, or colleagues we
trust. It is a wisdom of the instantaneous, which requires time and information rather than knowledge; in traditional societies, for instance, it is
the elderly who are supposed to possess such wisdom.

Common sense stops when questioning begins. The only questions it
can face are those already solved in the stock of knowledge available to
individuals. Questions are rhetorical in the sense that they are answered
beforehand by ready-made and often inconsistent ideas and judgments.

The generality of commonsense "wisdom" is provided by groups of commonplaces, which are often contradictory in order to be adapted to a variety of situations, if not to all of them. Common sense can be as closed upon itself as an ideology (and, in fact, it is often ideological). But it is also an empirical knowledge to the extent that it is each time adapted to its object, even though it is only an answer to the specific problem in question. Common sense, when it relies on some ad hoc empirical, is circular: the answer it gives is only valid for a specific question and lacks all generality. Its labeling of a fact to explain already contains what to think of that fact; as a result, the question already embodies the solution to which it is only supposed to lead. Common sense judges, where the arbiter (and also science) would rather consider itself as questioning.

Science tests the qualification of the facts it studies and sees the labels given to them as questions or as hypotheses to test further with other facts. To describe is already to interpret, if not to explain.

If I raise the issue of the progress of history, for example, two questions are involved. The first bears on the fact itself: Is there such a fact? The second could be understood as raising the problem of causality: if we admit such a progress, the only interpretation left for the question must be that which requires the explanation of the fact. We can see the second reading at work in an issue like the one involved in the study of the problem of the French Revolution. Who would deny that it actually occurred? But what did exactly happen? In order to answer that question, one must already avail oneself of an account of the facts, which is also a description and not simply an explanation. Both are intertwined. Common sense conflates the two questions: the explanation is projected onto the fact in its very description. Science, on the contrary, severs both questions, even if the explanation that is sought eventually rebounds on the mere description of the *explanandum*.

The basic method followed by science consists of considering any explanatory account of a given problem as ad hoc, unless it applies to another fact, another question. An explanatory statement of a given fact is most likely to apply to the fact in question, since it has been produced for that purpose. The difficulty—and the task—lies in the possibility of using it for a question for which it was not designed. For instance, if there is progress in history, the explanation must account for other types of evolution. If we find an explanation which describes how the French Revolution actually took place, it also indirectly applies to other revolutions. The explanation B of A must be validated by something other than A, let us say C, and so forth. Science needs theories, where common sense can afford to be impressionistic or more or less inconsistent in its superficial systematicity. Such an approach, if it prevailed, would turn out to be nonempirical and closed, as ideologies are.

Experience, as much as logic, is a way of treating and testing alternatives, of eliminating them. Both are procedures of answering. The consequences of such work on alternatives are the traditional ones associated with scientific method—simplicity, fecundity, and theoretical systematicity. If B explains A and D, for which originally two distinct explanatory statements have been offered, B as a stronger explanation and will be then preferred. The explanatory chain A, B, C, D becomes a theory, and the theory is all the more fecund in that it generates fewer explanations for a wider area of facts, thereby letting them be grouped into a restricted number of classes of phenomena. Unity in grasping the phenomena ensues; light and heat become related, space-time and gravitation share the same root, and so on. All of this is well known, and it stems from the fact that scientific problematization complies with the law of dissociation described above. That law suggests compliance with the problematological difference: the question of fact relies on the acceptance of the fact, even as it questions it. Something must be out-of-the-question in the fact, and something else must be in question throughout. The answer sought nonetheless bears on the fact, and it has usually been called its *reason*. The only way to avoid circularity in this matter is to test the answer on other facts, i.e., on other questions.

Finally, what emerges here is a new vision of rationality, which broadens the traditional view. Answers are important, but they presuppose questioning, which is the real foundation. As such, questioning can be found in language, in science, and in all forms of reasoning, ranging from rhetoric to the most constrained forms of inference.

Notes

Chapter 1   The Birth of Propositionalism, and How Ontology Became Anthropology: Aristotle and Descartes

1. J.-M. Le Blond, *Logique et méthode chez Aristote,* 3d ed. (Paris: Vrin, 1973), 147.
2. R. Descartes, *Meditations of First Philosophy,* trans. J. Cottingham (Cambridge: Cambridge University Press, 1985), 30–31.
3. R. M. Albérès, *Métamorphoses du roman* (Paris: Albin Michel, 1966), 133.
4. R. Heyndels, *La pensée fragmentée* (Brussels: Mardaga, 1985), 22.
5. F. Van Rossum-Guyon, *Critique du roman* (Paris: Gallimard, 1970), 28.

Chapter 2   Rhetoric in the Twentieth Century: From Proposition to the Question

1. C. Brooke-Rose, *A Rhetoric of the Unreal* (Cambridge: Cambridge University Press, 1981), 3.
2. J. Naremore, *The World without a Self* (New Haven: Yale University Press, 1973), 28.
3. A. Ehrenzweig, *The Hidden Order of Art* (Berkeley and Los Angeles: University of California Press, 1971), 33–34.
4. J. Fekete, *The Structural Allegory* (Minneapolis: University of Minnesota Press, 1984), xxii.
5. B. Kawin, *The Mind of the Novel* (Princeton: Princeton University Press, 1982).
6. R. Langbaum, *The Mysteries of Identity* (Chicago: University of Chicago Press, 1977), 97.
7. F. Kafka, *Parables and Paradoxes* (New York: Schocken Books, 1975), 181.
8. For a fuller analysis of Kafka's *Prüfung,* see my essay "Kafka, or the Existentiality of Questioning," in *Questions and Questioning,* ed. M. Meyer (Berlin and New York: De Gruyter, 1988), 341–355.
9. M. Heidegger, *Nietzsche,* 1:471; as quoted in S. Rosen, *Nihilism* (New Haven: Yale University Press, 1969), 96.
10. R. Hanna, *Review of Metaphysics* (1983): 412.

11. "The technique of question and answer is of little value when we are concerned with a presentation of specialized theme addressed to an audience of experts, in physics, history, or law for example, since each discipline possesses a group of theses and methods which every specialist is supposed to acknowledge and which is rarely called into question. . . . It is, on the contrary, in the absence of recognized truths and theses that recourse to a dialectic of question and answer appears to be indispensable" (C. Perelman, *The Realm of Rhetoric* [Notre Dame: University of Notre Dame Press, 1982], 16).

12. On the problematological theory of literature, see M. Meyer, *Meaning and Reading* (Amsterdam: Benjamins, 1983).

13. A. Jefferson, *The Nouveau Roman and the Poetics of Fiction* (Cambridge: Cambridge University Press, 1980), 18.

14. Ibid., 19–20.

15. On the comparison between problematology and deconstruction, see the French version of *Meaning and Reading—Langage et littérature* (Paris: Presses Universitaires de France, 1993), 224–225.

16. Z. McKeon, *Novels and Arguments* (Chicago: University of Chicago Press, 1982), 40–41.

17. Ibid., 8.

18. Ibid., 16.

Chapter 4   Reasoning with Language

1. The germ of this notion was already to be found in the *Tractatus;* the questions being posed, although once resolved or dissolved, still remain the real problems fundamentally and inexpressibly tied to life, problems which no language can adequately capture, much less resolve. "We *feel* that, even if all possible scientific questions are answered, *our problem is still not touched at all.* Of course, in that case are no questions any more, and that is the answer" (L. Wittgenstein, *Notebooks, 1914–1916* [Oxford: Blackwell, 1979], 51).

2. On the five possibilities of dialectical interaction, see M. Meyer, "La conception problématologique du langage," in *L'interrogation: Langue française* (Paris: Larousse, 1981), 80–100.

3. Napoleon as real entity—what is that? The answer determines Napoleon in his reality, and we must apprehend him by means of answers. If it is a question about Peter, Paul, or Jack, then which Peter, Paul, or Jack? These beings are only real to me once this question is resolved. Judgment is generated, through interrogation, by resolving the question. The judgment answers a specific question.

4. See M. Meyer, *Découverte et justification en science* (Paris: Klincksieck, 1979), and also "Dialectique, rhétorique, herméneutique et questionnement," *Revue Internationale de Philosophie* 127/128 (1979): 145–177.

Chapter 5   How to Give Meaning with Words

1. J. Lyons, *Introduction to Theoretical Linguistics* (Cambridge: Cambridge University Press, 1968), 11.

2. Meyer, *Meaning and Reading,* 77–99.

3. L. Wittgenstein, *The Philosophical Grammar* (Oxford: Blackwell, 1965), §6.

4. See M. Meyer, "Problematology and Rhetoric," in *Practical Reasoning in Human Affairs,* ed. J. Golden and J. Pilotta (Dordrecht: Reidel, 1986), 119–152.

5. See M. Meyer, *De la problématologie* (Brussels: Mardaga, 1986; English translation forthcoming from the University of Chicago Press).

6. What Jean Cohen has called "Les théories de l'écart" in *La structure du langage poétique* (Paris: Flammarion, 1966), 21–99.

7. "The repertoire consists of all the familiar territory within the text. This may be in the form of references to earlier works, or to social and historical norms, or to the whole culture from which the test has emerged" (W. Iser, *The Act of Reading* [Baltimore: Johns Hopkins University Press, 1978], 69).

8. W. Iser, "The Reality of Fiction," *New Literary History* 7, no. 1 (1975): 2.

9. I. Calvino, *If on a Winter's Night a Traveller,* trans. W. Weaver (London: Picador, 1982), 15.

10. Ibid.

11. Ibid.

12. Ibid.

Chapter 6 The Rationality of Knowledge

1. See my *Découverte et justification en science,* 365.

2. P. Achinstein, *Concepts of Science* (Baltimore: Johns Hopkins University Press, 1968), 72–80.

3. K. Popper, *The Logic of Scientific Discovery,* 3d ed. (London: Hutchinson, 1968), 82.

4. G. Andersson, "Presuppositions, Problems, Progress," in *The Structure and Development of Science,* ed. G. Radnitzky and G. Andersson (Dordrecht: Reidel, 1979), 3.

5. C. Hempel, *The Philosophy of Natural Science* (Englewood Cliffs, N.J.: Prentice-Hall, 1966), 5.

6. An answer can also be rejected as answer; it can be put into question and thereby give rise to a new questioning process which increases science at large. Although based on a theory of questioning which remains implicit, the same idea can be found in the excellent book by Harold Brown, *Perception: Theory and Commitment* (Chicago: University of Chicago Press, 1977), 132–134.

7. Larry Laudan brings this difference implicitly into play when he argues that "if a problem can be characterized only within the language and the framework of a theory which purports to solve it, then clearly no competing theory could be said to solve the same problem. However, so long as the theoretical assumptions necessary to characterize the problem are different from the theories which attempt to solve it, then it is possible to show that the competing explanatory theories are addressing themselves to the same problem" (*Progress and Its Problems* [Berkeley and Los Angeles: University of California Press, 1977], 143). There is a difference between the language of problems and that of solutions, and accepting the presuppositions of a question is a matter of understanding and not of agreement, which is reserved for answers.

8. A remarkable exposition of Karl Popper's philosophy of science can be found in G. Radnitzky, "Popperian Philosophy of Science as an Antidote against Relativism," in *Essays in Memory of Imre Lakatos,* ed. R. Cohen et al. (Dordrecht: Reidel, 1976), 505–506. See also G. Radnitzky and G. Andersson, eds., *Progress and Rationality in Science* (Dordrecht: Reidel, 1978).

9. "Sir Karl has erred by transferring selected characteristics of everyday research to the occasional revolutionary episodes in which scientific advance is most obvious and by thereafter ignoring the everyday enterprise entirely. In particular, he has sought to solve the problem of theory choice during revolutions by logical criteria that are applicable in full only when a theory can already be presupposed" (T. Kuhn, "Logic of Discovery or Psychology of Research?" in *Criticism and the Growth of Knowledge,* ed. I. Lakatos and A. Musgrave [Cambridge: Cambridge University Press, 1970], 19). The logical criteria referred to concern the use of the

modus tollens, the basis for the falsification theory. Research, according to Popper, is clearly conceived according to the logicist's model; discovery is seen as a simple psychological process. Kuhn is right to point out that the logic of justification is a logic of experience and existence.

10. The book by Richard H. Brown, *A Poetic for Sociology: Toward a logic of discovery for the human sciences* (Cambridge: Cambridge University Press, 1977), 77–172, not only has an excellent title but illustrates this perfectly.

11. See F.C.S. Schiller, "Scientific Discovery and Logical Proof," in *Studies in the History and Method of Science,* ed. C. Singer (Oxford: Oxford University Press, 1917), 279.

12. M. Hesse, *Models and Analogies in Science* (Notre Dame: University of Notre Dame Press, 1966), 66.

Bibliography

Achinstein, P. *Concepts of Science*. Baltimore: Johns Hopkins University Press, 1968.

Albérès, R. M. *Métamorphoses du roman*. Paris: Albin Michel, 1966.

Andersson, G. "Presuppositions, Problems, Progress." In *The Structure and Development of Science*, edited by G. Radnitzky and G. Andersson. Dordrecht: Reidel, 1979.

Anscombre, J.-C., and O. Ducrot, *L'argumentation dans la langue*. Brussels: Mardaga, 1983.

Aristotle. *Complete Works*. Edited by J. Barnes. Princeton: Princeton University Press, 1985.

Belnap, N. "Questions, Answers, and Presuppositions." *Journal of Philosophy* 63 (1966): 609–611.

———. "Questions: Their presuppositions and how they fail to arise." In *The Logical Way of Doing Things*, edited by K. Lambert. New Haven: Yale University Press, 1969.

Brooke-Rose, C. *A Rhetoric of the Unreal*. Cambridge: Cambridge University Press, 1981.

Brown, H. *Perception: Theory and Commitment*. Chicago: University of Chicago Press, 1977.

Brown, R. *A Poetic for Sociology: Toward a logic of discovery for the human sciences*. Cambridge: Cambridge University Press, 1977.

Calvino, I. *If on a Winter's Night a Traveller*. Translated by W. Weaver. London: Picador, 1982.

Cohen, J. *La structure du langage poétique*. Paris: Flammarion, 1966.

Derrida, J. *Margins*. Chicago: University of Chicago Press, 1982.

———. *Of Grammatology*. Baltimore: Johns Hopkins University Press, 1976.

Descartes, R. *Meditations of First Philosophy*. Translated by J. Cottingham. Cambridge: Cambridge University Press, 1985.

Ehrenzweig, A. *The Hidden Order of Art*. Berkeley and Los Angeles: University of California Press, 1971.

Fekete, J. *The Structural Allegory*. Minneapolis: University of Minnesota Press, 1984.

Foucault, M. *The Order of Things*. New York: Vintage, 1970.

Goody, E. *Questions and Politeness*. Cambridge: Cambridge University Press, 1978.

Grize, J. B. *De la logique à l'argumentation*. Geneva: Droz, 1982.

Hanna, R. Review of *The Realm of Rhetoric*, by Chaim Perelman. *Review of Metaphysics* (1983).

Heidegger, M. *Nietzsche*. 2 vols. Pfullingen: Neske, 1961.

Hempel, C. *The Philosophy of Natural Science*. Englewood Cliffs, N.J.: Prentice-Hall, 1966.

Hesse, M. *Models and Analogies in Science*. Notre Dame: University of Notre Dame Press, 1966.

Heyndels, R. *La pensée fragmentée*. Brussels: Mardaga, 1985.

Hintikka, J. *The Semantics of Questions and the Questions of Semantics*. Amsterdam: North-Holland, 1976.

Iser, W. *The Act of Reading*. Baltimore: Johns Hopkins University Press, 1978.

———. "The Reality of Fiction." *New Literary History* 7, no. 1 (1975): 7–38.

Janicaud, D. *La puissance du rationnel*. Paris: Gallimard, 1985.

Jefferson, A. *The Nouveau Roman and the Poetics of Fiction*. Cambridge: Cambridge University Press, 1980.

Kafka, F. *Parables and Paradoxes*. New York: Schocken Books, 1975.

Kawin, B. *The Mind of the Novel*. Princeton: Princeton University Press, 1982.

Kuhn, T. "Logic of Discovery or Psychology of Research?" In *Criticism and the Growth of Knowledge*, edited by I. Lakatos and A. Musgrave, 1–23. Cambridge: Cambridge University Press, 1970.

Lacan, J. *Ecrits*. Paris: Le Seuil, 1966.

Langbaum, R. *The Mysteries of Identity*. Chicago: University of Chicago Press, 1977.

Laudan, L. *Progress and Its Problems*. Berkeley and Los Angeles: University of California Press, 1977.

Le Blond, J.-M. *Logique et méthode chez Aristote*. 3d ed. Paris: Vrin, 1973.

Lyons, J. *Introduction to Theoretical Linguistics*. Cambridge: Cambridge University Press, 1968.

McKeon, Z. *Novels and Arguments*. Chicago: University of Chicago Press, 1982.

Meyer, M. "La conception problématologique du langage." *L'interrogation: Langue française*, 80–100. Paris: Larousse, 1981.

———. *Découverte et justification en science*. Paris: Klincksieck, 1979.

———. *De la problématologie*. Brussels: Mardaga, 1986.

———. "Dialectique, rhétorique, herméneutique et questionnement." *Revue Internationale de Philosophie* 127/128 (1979): 145–177.

———. *From Logic to Rhetoric*. Amsterdam: Benjamins, 1986.

———. "The Interrogative Theory of Meaning and Reference." In *Questions and Questioning*, edited by M. Meyer. Berlin and New York: De Gruyter, 1988.

———. "Kafka, or the Existentiality of Questioning." In *Questions and Questioning*, edited by M. Meyer, 341–355. Berlin and New York: De Gruyter, 1988.

———. *Meaning and Reading*. Amsterdam: Benjamins, 1983.

————. "On Meaning and Reading: An Exchange with Iser." *Revue Internationale de Philosophie* 3/4 (1987): 414–420.

————. "Pour une rhétorique de la raison." *Revue Internationale de Philosophie* 155 (1985): 289–302.

————. "Problematology and Rhetoric." In *Practical Reasoning in Human Affairs,* edited by J. Golden and J. Pilotta. Dordrecht: Reidel, 1986.

Naremore, J. *The World without a Self.* New Haven: Yale University Press, 1973.

Perelman, C. *The New Rhetoric and the Humanities.* Dordrecht: Reidel, 1979.

————. *The Realm of Rhetoric.* Notre Dame: University of Notre Dame Press, 1982.

Popper, K. *The Logic of Scientific Discovery.* 3d ed. London: Hutchinson, 1968.

Radnitzky, G. "Popperian Philosophy of Science as an Antidote against Relativism." In *Essays in Memory of Imre Lakatos,* edited by R. Cohen et al., 505–547. Dordrecht: Reidel, 1976.

Radnitzky, G., and G. Andersson, eds. *Progress and Rationality in Science.* Dordrecht: Reidel, 1978.

Rosen, S. *Nihilism.* New Haven: Yale University Press, 1969.

Schiller, F.C.S. "Scientific Discovery and Logical Proof." In *Studies in the History and Method of Science,* edited by C. Singer, 235–291. Oxford: Oxford University Press, 1917.

Van Rossum–Guyon, F. *Critique du roman.* Paris: Gallimard, 1970.

Wittgenstein, L. *Notebooks, 1914–1916.* Oxford: Blackwell, 1979.

————. *The Philosophical Grammar.* Oxford: Blackwell, 1965.

Index